Self-Empowerment·
Have the Life You ꓘ

Self-Empowerment: Have the Life You Want!

*How to close the gap between how life is,
and how you would like it to be
in important areas of life such as
Mental Health, Health, Relationships, Career,
Finances, Family, Community, and Spirituality*

*The lessons I've learned from my clients
in over 18 years as a psychotherapist and life coach*

Ken Howard, LCSW

NOTE TO READERS

This publication contains the ideas and opinions of its author. It is intended to provide helpful and educational material on the subjects addressed in the publication. It is sold with the understanding that the author and publisher are not engaged in rendering mental health, medical, health, financial, or any other kind of personal professional services in the book. The reader should consult his or her mental health, medical, health, financial, or other appropriate and competent professional before adopting any of the suggestions in this book or drawing inferences from it. The author and publisher specifically disclaim all responsibility for any loss, liability, or risk, personal or otherwise, which is incurred as a consequence, directly or indirectly, of the use and application of any of the contents of this book or its excerpts and derivatives, in any media.

All case studies are fiction, based on an amalgam of cases seen in actual clinical practice.

Self-published by the author at www.LuLu.com

First Printing, July, 2011

ISBN #: 978-0-557-57259-5

Front and back cover designs by Sherice Jacob, www.ielectrify.com

Cover photo by John Skalicky, www.skalickyphoto.com

Hair by Jena Leavitt

The author is available for motivational speaking for your live event. To book an event, contact the author at the address below or at 310-726-4357 or at www.HaveTheLifeYouWant.com.

Sign up for updates and additional information at www.HaveTheLifeYouWant.com.

Follow the podcast episodes of "Have the Life You Want with Ken Howard, LCSW" at iTunes.com, Zune.com, PodcastAlley.com, or your favorite podcast provider.

Ken Howard, LCSW
Counseling – Psychotherapy – Coaching – Consulting
8430 Santa Monica Boulevard, Suite 100
West Hollywood, CA 90069

For Hunny...

Contents

Acknowledgements

To all of my teachers, supervisors, mentors, colleagues, and inspirations, who each imparted many hours of their own support, education, experience, and wisdom to me, without whom this book would not have been possible:

Joan C. Bedinger

Susan Holt, MA, CDVC

Michael Shernoff, MSW, LCSW

Maggie Magee, Ph.D., LCSW

Kathleen Haugh, LCSW

Frank Paradise, LCSW

Lisa Valtierra

Eric G. Bing, MD, Ph.D.

James Babl, Ph.D.

Brian Miller, Ph.D.

Brian Gold, Ph.D.

Dee Bridgewater, Ph.D.

Rick Hyman, Ph.D., MFT

Tony Zimbardi, Psy.D., MFT

Mickie Robbins, MFT

Tom Donohoe, MBA

Sandra Rogers, MFT

Bethany Marshall, Psy.D., Ph.D., MFT

Barry Cardiner, MFT

Barbara Crofford, LCSW

Michael Kaltenbach, LCSW

Geoffrey Milam, LCSW

Joey Sarcoz, MA

Joe Kort, Ph.D., LMSW

Richard Gollance, LCSW

Jonathan Lynch, MFT

Greg Cason, Ph.D.

Adrian Miles

Sheri Tor

Jirka Ambroz

Gregory Cox

Nigel Campbell

Bernard Bierman, MD

Tom Kerrihard, MD

Patricia Bowers

Sherice Jacob

Robert Decker

Susan Giurleo, Ph.D.

Karyl Draper, LCSW

Julie Steres, MFT

Glenda F. Camp, Ph.D.

Gregory Herek, Ph.D.

Keith Young, MD

Steven Schenkel, MD

Michael Gottlieb, MD

Peter Ruane, MD

Charles Skiba, DO

Essie Seck, Ph.D.

Casey Truffo, MFT   Linda Poverny, Ph.D.

Lynn Grodzki, LCSW   Jill Howard Church, MA

Juliet Austin, MA   Michael C. Ryan

With deep gratitude to Dan Kael, Bill Lockard, Sherice Jacob, Tom Kerrihard, MD, Bernard Bierman, MD, and Michael C. Ryan for their generous gift of time and expert advice in reviewing the manuscript. Your brilliance is profoundly appreciated!

With affection and thanks to all my family, especially my sister, Jill Howard Church (who writes way more better than I do), and to my husband, Michael C. Ryan.

And my fondest gratitude to my clients who inspired the amalgamations that became the case studies – who must remain anonymous – and with my apologies for changing your genders, careers, and other identifying facts to protect your confidentiality. It is an honor and a privilege to know each of you.

Preface

One could say that this is a book about teaching. But is it my teaching others, based on the study of human behavior, theories of human development, and the profound psychological hypotheses of the great masters? Or is it relating what my patients/clients (I will use those terms interchangeably in this book) have taught me, over more than 18 years of clinical practice as a psychotherapist? I think I have helped them in various ways to cope with the variety of life challenges they have presented me. But I also think they have taught me: about the resilience of the human spirit, the complexity of how the human mind and heart grow and develop over time, and the many ways that brave people release old fears and find new ways to raise their quality of life. Without these many lessons, taught over thousands of fifty-minute therapy sessions and ninety-minute group therapy sessions, this book would never have been possible.

Some of the ways I continue to help people in my practice is to use my own memory – (even, as actors would say, my own "sense memory", which is a memory laden with emotion) or the methods other clients have used to cope, survive, and thrive, and seeing if those methods might apply to a new person facing a similar problem. Over time, the "database" of observed coping strategies grows. I hope that each patient who overcomes a problem realizes that they are leaving a legacy within the walls of my office that may somehow invisibly inspire the next patient who comes along with a similar predicament, telling them that they are not alone, there is hope, things can and do get better, with hard work, time and healing.

This book is also perhaps to teach those who have never been in therapy or coaching more about these professions. Maybe by learning more about what therapists do, it will make the process seem a bit less scary, reduce the (frustrating) stigma some still attach to seeking such services, and make those who were too afraid of seeking a therapist gain the bravery it takes to contact one. I'm always humbled by a story of a new patient that I had a couple of years ago. On his first session, when I was asking how he found me, he admitted, "I had your business card on my desk for a year before I got the courage to call you." I was moved by this, because while I don't think of myself as a scary person, I know the prospect of seeing a therapist can be scary. I am honored by someone who overcomes such trepidation. I always strive to do my best work with each client, but that story made me silently remind myself of the need for therapists to commit themselves to doing their best work with each new patient; it's the least I can do to honor his commitment to the process. I wanted to be "worth the wait" for him.

When someone asks me what I do for a living, sometimes, if they catch me in the right playful mood, I'll say I'm an anesthesiologist. Not (hopefully!) because I make people fall asleep, but because I am there to help them reduce pain. I'm also a gardener – I make things (people) grow. I'm also a little bit of a slave-driver. Sometimes a parent. Sometimes a sparring-partner. But always, caring. One of my early teachers, Susan Holt, used to say, "You pay for my skills; you get my caring for free."

I hope this book sells a lot of copies. I admit it. I hope hundreds of thousands of people read it and enjoy it. I would be thrilled for them (the royalties wouldn't be so bad, either – the section on Prosperity will explain more about this!). But there are lots of ways in this lifetime that one could have money – a real estate agent, a stock broker, maybe a movie producer. But as noble as those professions are (I hear about them from my clients in those fields), they wouldn't be as fulfilling to me as what I do now as a therapist and coach. I've heard that one of the rewards of teaching school (it's certainly not the salaries) is the satisfaction of seeing the kids grow and thrive, and to see what they become, hoping that perhaps you had something to do with their successful outcomes. The same could be said of therapists. Helping my clients overcome obstacles, heal past wounds, and go on to survive and thrive is more rewarding than anything else I can think of that a person can do for a living. Therapy may be how I make my living, but what I enjoy most is seeing my clients make the therapeutic process work for them; going from unhappy to happy, amateur to seasoned professional, frustrated to fulfilled, fearful to confident, addicted to liberated, damaged to healed, demoralized to confident, chaotic to calm. Over and over again.

With that sense of pride, hope, and joy in what I do, I share the following ideas with you. I want you to enjoy what you read here.

I want you to implement some of the suggestions in it. I want you to think and behave in different, better, and more empowered ways as a result of what you read here. And I want you... to have the life you want!

West Hollywood, CA
May, 2011

What is having the life you want?

At my live seminar version of, "Have the Life You Want," I start by asking the audience to ask themselves what "having the life you want" means for them. What do they think of? If I could do anything, what would I do? If I could be anything, what would I be? If I could go anywhere, where would I go? If I could have anything, what would I have? Part of improving life starts with assessing how your life is, right now.

When most people think about that, they start to have a vision of "peaks and valleys" in their heads. They have a great spouse or partner, but their health isn't good. Or they have a great house, but their job just plain sucks. Or they have a great job, house, health, and kids, but their relationship is not what they want. There was a joke on "Friends" that said you couldn't have a good job, apartment, and relationship all at the same time. Now, that's a little fatalistic and perhaps negative, but many people identified with the sentiment that it's hard to get all of the domains of your life going well at the same time. But it is possible – which is perhaps the most important first step there is – BELIEVING that it is possible, not only to "cope", but to "thrive", in all areas of your life.

To me, having the life you want is about thinking how your life is, how you would like it to be, and then working to close the gap between the two. Closing the gap means changing the way you think or behave in various areas of life. What would I need to do to close the gap? What changes in my beliefs would it require? What resources would I need? What limits do I need to set? Who would I need support from? What would I need to get realistic about? What would I need to sacrifice? What would I have to let go of? What would I need to embrace?

Having the life you want means not just enjoying the aspects of your life that are going particularly well – like winning the lottery and paying off all your debts and having financial security – it's also about raising the bar in a number of areas. If we slice up the pie of our lives, we find life falls into important domains for our consciousness and attention. In my observation in my practice, it seems these domains fall into categories, such as Mental Health, Health, Relationships, Work, Finances, Prosperity, Family, Community, and Spirituality.

These domains become familiar when we think of the ideal of the "well-rounded person." The "Renaissance Man" (or woman). When we think of colleges that propound a "well-rounded" liberal arts education curriculum, they are designing programs that include exposure to the student of many subjects as courses of study, with the idea that a diversity of knowledge makes for a strong knowledge base with which to go out into the world and "conquer" it. We never know when we might need to make a mathematical calculation, calm ourselves by remembering a quote of philosophy, or apply a theory to a business task. It is implied in such curricula that if we know some (or even quite a bit) about a lot of subjects, we are somehow better equipped to face the world and gain a high quality of life.

The same could be said about the living skills inherent in life's "domains." Much of the work that is performed in therapy, by both therapist and client, is about inquiry and assessment of these various life domains. And the domains that are the least "mastered" are usually where the greatest source of heartache and frustration lies. It is the task, then, to learn (via the process of therapy) how to master, or at least improve, our skills in working in those domains, utilizing the strengths we have in other domains for assistance.

Oh, is that all? How simple! Anyone can do that!

Actually, that's not as daunting as it sounds. We'll look at each of those domains in this book to illustrate a perspective on how each part fits with the others.

Another element to having the life you want is to reduce the "bad" in your life – symptoms, frustrations, fears, and challenges – and increase the "good" in your life – joys, rewards, satisfaction, and relief. It is generally understood (though hard to find explicitly) that the reason why insurance companies often pay for psychotherapy is because they recognize therapy as a means to keep people functioning, healthy, and productive. Society has a vested interest in keeping its citizens as highly functioning as possible. Highly functioning people aren't on welfare or disability rolls. Highly functioning people pay taxes. Highly functioning people protect national security. We need to have our citizenry as capable as possible – and therapy (in addition to medical care) is one way to achieve that. In the age of "managed care" (some patients and providers would say, in frustration, "mis-managed care"), the insurance companies want patients to be as well as possible, as soon as possible and at the minimal possible cost. Patients want to get better quickly, too, but in the case of psychotherapy, solid and enduring gains (as opposed to superficial and transient ones) often take time. That said, my particular style of psychotherapy does tend to "push" the patient/client a bit, because working in specific and goal-directed ways often results in regular, measurable, and appreciable growth and improvement.

It is this dually purposed goal of reducing the "bad" and increasing the "good" that characterizes any given therapy session. Either one of these can contribute to raising quality of life. And it is this process of *improving quality of life by troubleshooting challenges and building adaptive coping skills in each of life's domains* that I mean when I speak of "have the life you want."

Mental Health

Defining Mental Health

Considering the concept of self-empowerment in "Mental Health" is a complex task. Immediately, the term "mental health" for some people can arouse anxiety, in the sense that they think that a poor mental health means someone who is crazy, out of control, psychotic, burdensome, fearsome, and a whole host of negative connotations. As much as Hollywood has given us wonderful gifts of entertainment to cherish through the ages, they have sometimes promoted the stigma of anything other than pristine mental health. Movies like *Psycho* and *Silence of the Lambs* teach that people with mental illness are to be feared like no other kind of person on Earth. Yet these audiences usually don't know, as the National Alliance for the Mentally Ill likes to remind the public, that people with severe mental illness are far more often the victims of crime than they are the perpetrators of it. I've worked with people with severe mental illness in a psychiatric hospital and in local psychiatric rehabilitation programs, and conditions such as Schizophrenia or severe Bipolar Disorder can be heartbreaking in their severity. But even then, there is treatment, coping, and adaptation, called Psychosocial Rehabilitation, that helps these people develop independent living skills and improve their quality of life. Yet when we discuss mental health here, I'm really addressing readers who are not necessarily suffering with a major mental illness such as Schizophrenia, but more of the average person who has less severe conditions, or average "ups and downs" in their mental health. Yet to consider what this concept of mental health is, we should define it.

There are perhaps too many ways to define mental health. I think it can be confused with feelings of ideal comfort, relaxation, happiness, contentment, or joy. But mental health is perhaps the capacity to handle many different feelings and impulses and still maintain some personal equilibrium and social grace. Immanuel Kant's "Rules for Happiness" are "something to do, someone to love, and something to hope for." I think also that mental health is supported by just being near the things we love – the people, work, hobbies, cultural rituals, pastimes, and anything that brings us joy to see, do, or just be close to. Being near the things we love, whatever they are, can be a buoyant to our mood.

When you are not feeling well in terms of your mental health, ask yourself, What do I need to be nearer to in order to feel better? Sometimes you need a good cry, sometimes to go watch a funny TV show, sometimes to go home, sometimes to have a hug, and sometimes a day to yourself to just go to the mall and wander around. Even having this book handy might provide an immediate occasional boost, as needed. In my practice, we discuss what mental health means to each client, and what would have to change about themselves, the people around them, or their circumstances, in order to achieve a sense of well-being beyond their current state.

Mental Health Issues—Symptoms

Mental health can be defined as the "absence of symptoms." It's hard to say we are in the zone of pristine mental health if we are suffering from the symptoms that come with depression. These symptoms may include persistent and unrelenting sad mood, hopelessness, futility about the future, lack of pleasure in the things we used to enjoy (or not even doing the things we used to enjoy), fatigue, problems falling asleep or staying asleep, self-isolation, irritability, crying more often, and persistent negative thoughts about ourselves, the world around us, or our future. Depression must be distinguished from normal periods of sad mood, which we all have at times. Clinical depression is stronger, more pervasive, and less responsive to actions that normally raise our mood. It is perhaps the most common disorder that I see in clients – and the most common clinical diagnosis I give. Depression can vary widely in its severity, from a mild case where the person doesn't even seek treatment, to the major case where a person must seek permanent disability benefits. I've always said that if the Eskimos have dozens of words for "snow," then therapists need dozens of words for "depression" to describe the many subtle and even insidious manifestations it takes. For many clients in my practice, the combination of therapy and medication brings much improved outcomes in managing depression, even if it tends to recur.

Anxiety also can keep us out of our pristine mental health zone. Anxiety is marked by excessive worrying, ruminating, fear, fidgeting, tummy trouble, diarrhea, obsessive thoughts, and self-isolation.

Obsessions and compulsions can take us out of that zone, and can be defined as "having" to arrange our physical belongings in a certain order, counting things irrationally, touching or not touching objects in a certain way, or the inability to stop thinking of a certain person or thing. Anger is another condition that can work against us, such as paying the price for not controlling our aggressive impulses such that we harm ourselves via embarrassment, or others by frightening or alienating them, or even doing physical harm to objects or others.

Fatigue can be a sign of impaired mental health all on its own. While this is more of a physical symptom that can accompany colds, flu, Chronic Fatigue Syndrome, HIV, cancer, or other illnesses, fatigue can also be a certain "mental fatigue" that is related to depression but can also be a symptom of chronic stress.

Fear is another impediment to mental health – anticipating a negative outcome of something we are invested in or care about. We cannot be givers and receivers of "good energy" and into the "green zone" of life, functioning as our best selves, if we are living in fear.

It's interesting to note how physical pain can be an impediment to mental health. Few people know that living in chronic pain can be a trigger for depression, or even suicidality (Clara Blandick, the actress who played Auntie Em in *The Wizard of Oz*, committed suicide over her inability to obtain relief from severe and deteriorating arthritis pain).

One could also say that self-empowerment in mental health is living a life in the absence of addictions, whether these are chemical (such as alcohol, nicotine, crystal methamphetamine, cocaine, heroin, prescription opiates, prescription tranquilizers) or behavioral (like spending, eating, working, gambling, or sex). While an active addiction is working in our lives, we cannot reach the "zone" of optimum functioning for ourselves, our relationships, or our work. Addictions stand between us and our "Muse" with life (Muses are the Greek goddesses who inspire the creation of art and literature). I think much of the recovering addict's work is doing whatever they need to do to liberate themselves from the tyranny of an addiction, where cognitions, behaviors, and social support (and for some, spirituality) combine to achieve sobriety.

Another definition of mental health on which I work with my clients relates to *doing what you love*. This is perhaps one of the most important existential questions that a person can ask about his life: Am I doing what I love? This can be in your personal life – with relationships and hobbies – or in your professional life. Perhaps the most "mentally healthy" people in the world are those who feel that they are truly doing what they love the majority of the time. Finding what this is for you, and finding a way to get it, is often the work of therapy. Mastering self-empowerment can help get you there.

I don't think we can be self-empowered for optimum mental health without developing a positive Sense of Self. How do you feel about you? How do others feel about you? What kind of feedback do you get about who you are and what you do? One of the most challenging aspects of my work is frustration that I have meeting and working with wonderful people who don't think of themselves as wonderful – they can hardly see anything good in themselves at all. This is when we work on their self-esteem as an important component of their therapy, regardless of any other treatment goals they set for themselves. Without a positive sense of self, it's hard to do your best work, form your best relationships, or get into that wonderful "zone" of being your best self.

Self-empowerment in mental health is not just about how we feel about ourselves. It can also be about cultivating good relationships. The saying goes, "No one is an island." Every one of us needs supportive relationships surrounding us, like the spokes of a wheel, to make that wheel spin. We need to see ourselves mirrored in others in order to orient us in the world. We need each other literally to exist. Prime mental health occurs when we have cultivated positive relationships with others who are our colleagues at work or in another vocational activity (such as volunteer work or philanthropic work), our friends, and perhaps most importantly in our spouse/partner. Something that I learned doing research with people who were both homeless and severely mentally ill was that it was not just the lack of a domicile and the presence of a mental illness that impeded the lives of these people, but it was also a social isolation – a "dis-affiliation" of the normal social bonds that most people function with (Grigsby et al. 1990). When we think of the homeless person with a severe (often untreated) mental illness, we see them as a loner and cut off from the rest of the world. This is part of that pathology. Perhaps less severely, the average person is out of the "optimal zone" when they are not sufficiently "plugged in" to the human resources around them that give life meaning, purpose, and "spice."

Another signal of good mental health involves achieving an optimal balance in several areas. We must balance the issues of Work versus Home, and attention to our Self versus Others. If one of these is out of balance, we get out of our optimal zone. If we emphasize work, we might get kudos and accolades from a boss and coworkers, prizes, raises, promotions, prestige, recognition, and a high salary. But if we do this to the expense of our health, or our mental health (stress, fatigue, joylessness), we haven't achieved as much as we thought. If we have an optimal home life with good personal relationships, hobbies, a nice place to live, and lots of fun, but we neglect to perform adequately in our work life, plan our careers, and develop our Professional Self, then we can't really make it in a society that demands that able-bodied people work. One of the things that is part of my initial assessment with my clients is to see to what degree their home life is balanced with their work life. In most cases, we need to work to balance this by strengthening one or the other.

Similar to doing what you love, another hallmark of mental health is what I call "creating new good memories." Think about your life thus far – what do you recall as being some of the happiest times of your life? What comes to mind? Where were you? Who was with you? What were you doing? What was fun about it? How do you feel when you recall these times? If you're like most people, you just smiled a bit. It's a mood-buoyant to recall good memories. And how do we make good memories? By doing what we love and being with people we care about.

As much as these positive attributes contribute to our overall mental health, it's also important to "clear the wreckage" as the axiom in Alcoholics Anonymous says. In order to have optimal functioning and be in our good zone mentally, we need to have resolved and coped with past hurts, abuses, and negative or traumatic experiences. Negative experiences such as these "pour dirt" into our souls, and we need to have a way of cleaning it out. Often the goals of therapy can include processing (talking with emotional expression and a kind of catharsis) such experiences, including what happened, when, where, by whom, and how we felt about it, what we did about it then, and what we must do about it now.

Just after 9/11, many of my clients had to process what this experience meant for them in order to make sense of it existentially. Some were angry, some were sad, some made macabre jokes, others feigned indifference. But all of them were trying to cope with something that was part of our collective experience in our culture and in our times. Some clients have processed experiences of verbal, physical, and sexual abuse from their childhoods or early adolescence. Others have processed traumas such as being diagnosed with a serious illness, experiencing an accident, surviving a natural disaster, or losing a loved one. Some of my clients have experienced multiple traumas, or a combination of circumstances so severe it defies comprehension that so much can happen to one person. As painful as it can be to recall and process these experiences, doing this work provides a catharsis and an opportunity for healing of the soul that then allows for that person to heal, grow, and thrive into a new zone of self-empowerment in mental health.

Challenges: Mental Health

Self-empowerment when it comes to mental health is understanding that our emotions are messages that we must respond to (not just "react" to). Emotions are a tool for us to use, to make sense of the world around us, and to give us a sense of who we are in it. Emotions are a sign that something needs our attention and sometimes our intervention.

If we are overwhelmed with the many symptoms and manifestations of depression, anxiety, or myriad other psychiatric conditions, we are not self-empowered. We are in need of external resources, such as a psychotherapist and/or a psychiatrist (a Medical Doctor (MD) who prescribes medications especially for psychiatric disorders).

But even if a person does not have a severe disorder such as a Major Depressive Disorder, Generalized Anxiety Disorder, or Panic Disorder, when our mental health is not good, we can be "not" self-empowered because our emotions are "ruling" us, instead of the other way around. It's like the tail is wagging the dog. We feel helpless, at the mercy of our emotions, and feel that an outside force is oppressing us and keeping us from our best life's good. This is an illusion, and we must not buy in to the helplessness thinking that may tempt us.

I worked with a man who verbally abused his partner. In therapy, I confronted him on the destructive nature of this habit, which was his choice. He defended himself that he "couldn't help it" and I confronted that, too. He absolutely had a choice in his expression and language, and how and who it was directed at, and with responsibility for the effect of his behavior on others. The idea that one is "helpless" to their emotions is a fallacy. We might be wracked with grief at a severe loss, and feel the emotional pain of this deeply. But is entirely up to us on what we do with those emotions in adaptive coping. We could stay home, become lazy, and gain a ton of weight, wallowing in our own self-pity. Or, we could seek out a community support group and talk about our feelings that will lead to healing after a traumatic loss. We have choices. A good tip when feeling strong emotions is asking yourself, "What can I do about this?" and then brainstorm a list of options that begin with, "I could...."

Mental Health: Medication

One of the biggest pitfalls to self-empowerment that I see in daily clinical practice are those people who approach the use of medications with what I think is an unjustified level of guardedness and suspicion. I've worked with people who will smoke pot, snort cocaine, and toss back all kinds of alcohol, or even smoke, and they will say, "Oh! I don't even like to take aspirin!" Meanwhile, they are severely depressed, on the verge of being fired due to depression symptoms, or having their relationship crumble or have their children taken away, but oh, Lordy, don't anyone suggest that they have a psychiatric evaluation for the use of an antidepressant medication. Why is this? My opinion is that it has something to do with how adults learn and how adults form their opinions for or against something. Plus, I think there is quite a bit of social marketing at play. The corporations who make all kinds of stuff that is not all that good for you – or even downright bad for you – spend millions of dollars every year to make their unhealthy products somehow normal or palatable to the buying public. Meanwhile, other products (including medications) don't really "get through" to the public. The recent television ads for anti-depressant medications are making some headway about educating the public about what these medicines are, and what they are used for, but there is a long way to go. People really need to understand these "mysterious" and stigmatized medications just like they understand aspirin or penicillin.

The field of psychiatry must take some of the blame for the modern suspicion, though, however unreasonable, exaggerated or unfounded it may be. As recently as the 1970's, and certainly before then, psychiatry and the mental health field were notorious for denying patient's rights. Many, many years ago, some patients were held in almost dungeon-like "snake pits," and more recently in unethical institutions under horribly inhuman conditions. Movies such as "One Flew Over the Cuckoo's Nest" depict such patient abuse, and I think their impact has intimidated the average consumer about seeking psychiatric services ever since. In reality, it just doesn't work that way anymore. The National Alliance for the Mentally Ill (NAMI) certainly could give examples from its member families of hospitals, institutions, and programs that still violate patient's rights, but these are increasingly uncommon, and there is recourse now if a patient suffers abuse. Most facilities are required by law to publicly display a list of Patients' Rights on the walls of their facility, or give a handout listing these at the time of patient admission. Part of NAMI's advocacy is to support families with a mentally ill member, and to advocate for their appropriate care.

I've worked with clients who have been so depressed that they will tolerate feelings of wanting to kill themselves, but will still resist having an evaluation from a psychiatrist for medication. Their fears are outside the proportion of the risks. It is true that many clients have some side-effects from some of the most commonly prescribed anti-depressant medications (delayed ejaculation in sex, and perhaps a somewhat diminished libido, or "sex drive", are fairly common, but by no means universal to everyone). But relatively mild side-effects like delayed time in achieving orgasm (which some guys might find desirable) pale in comparison to the suffering of someone who is truly clinically depressed.

Psychiatrists are, relatively, a rare medical specialty, so their initial evaluation fees can seem high. Some providers bill insurance directly and some do not. But I prefer that anyone who needs an evaluation for any psychiatric condition (Major Depression, Generalized Anxiety Disorder, Insomnia, Obsessive-Compulsive Disorder, Attention-Deficit Disorder, Panic Disorder, Agoraphobia, etc.) be seen by a psychiatrist who treats these kinds of conditions all day, every day, as opposed to a general practitioner who might only deal with these things occasionally. Psychiatry is really an art and a science, and sometimes trial-and-error to find the type, dosage, or combination of medications that will bring the response that the patient desires – usually meaning the resolution of most or all symptoms, or at least making them more manageable. And unlike taking an antibiotic that may be effective in 99 percent of cases, working with psychotropic medications requires more finesse. I always say that a good psychiatrist is like a good chef, seasoning a stew – but he or she is really working with very gently manipulating the neurotransmitters in the brain with a "psychopharmacological intervention" that will bring about the desired subjective state in the patient – less depressed, more active, more motivated, less anxious, more positive, more restful, less lethargic, less irritable, less fearful, more focused, etc.

It doesn't help that myths, mis-information, and downright undermining of the psychiatric profession exist, for various reasons such as fear/mistrust, to commercial competition for other types of services. A certain former heart-throb actor has been known to publicly denigrate another star who has publicly spoken of the use of psychiatric medications, when they have no more than a high school education and are grossly unqualified to discuss the matter. Certain cult-style "religions" will actively attack the entire field of psychiatry (that's a pretty comprehensive target), so that people will seek out their services and pay them lots of money to "cure" them instead. You have to look at motives (and no, I don't get any kind of commissions from sending my therapy clients for a medication evaluation or from the sale of psychotropic medications). My bias is, however, in favor of using various psychiatric medications when you need them, because I have seen hundreds or thousands of clients at this point get a new lease on life when they have had a good response to a medication. I don't want anyone to suffer needlessly, if a medication could help them get their life back. It's lovely to see when this happens, which is fairly often. Therapy can do things medication can't do, but medication can do some things, I believe, that therapy can't do (some therapists would definitely disagree with me on this, and part of what makes this discussion complex is that you can have very well-informed people disagreeing professionally to a strong degree.) I believe that therapists should "start where the patient is," and strategize his or her treatment plan together.

Mental Health Finances

In the United States, psychotherapy is seen as perhaps a luxury, in that health insurance companies are increasingly resistant to paying reimbursement for it, in any way that is commensurate with the value of a licensed psychotherapist's professional services. For many people, making the sacrifice to pay for therapy privately means giving up spending that money on other things, but everyone must decide what is right for them on how they spend their resources in exchange for goods and services of perceived value. For some, no amount of personal re-budgeting can make therapy affordable. For most of these truly low-income people, there are publicly funded medical clinics or local mental health centers, funded by both Federal and state monies, collected from taxes. No one should feel that therapy services are inaccessible to them until they have researched and explored every available option in their own community.

By working to reduce the "bad" and increase the "good," and by avoiding some of these pitfalls, a person can be well on their way to self-empowerment in mental health.

Mental Health

Case Study: "Richard"

Richard was a twenty-one-year-old college student who came to see me in my private practice, funded by an allowance from his parents who lived out of state. He had done some online research, and had read some of my writings about Obsessive-Compulsive Disorder. He came to see me to learn more, as he had been suffering for several years with OCD symptoms where he felt compelled to say out loud, or at least think to himself, certain prayers. He believed that failing to do so would mean he would unconsciously "sell his soul to the Devil." Only the recitation ritual would absolve him. Simultaneously, he was in acute grief following the breakup of his relationship with Alice, who had moved to Los Angeles with him. His parents had been very supportive of Richard's relationship. But the extreme religiosity of Richard's upbringing in a conservative evangelical sect took its toll on Richard's young and somewhat vulnerable self-esteem. Combined with a family history of OCD (which is known to be genetic), his compulsions manifested with a persecutory religiosity theme.

My interventions with Richard largely used Cognitive-Behavioral Therapy (CBT) to address Richard's OCD. CBT instructs the patient on different ways to re-interpret the compulsions, and see them not as a product of "the Devil," but a product merely of OCD as a mental disorder, along with a game plan of how to resist and let go of compulsions. In addition, Richard needed encouragement to connect more with other friends his age, for validation, companionship, and a sense of belonging. Slowly, he built his self-esteem by forming close bonds with other young people. Like many people with OCD, Richard's commitment to his work as a designer was exceptional, but also all-consuming. He needed interventions to stop work at times, and to skip doing work at times when he needed appropriate rest (meal times, sleeping, and at least some recreational activity, alone or with peers).

Over time, Richard became self-empowered to understand what it's like to be a person living successfully with OCD, and how to cope with the fact that it is usually a chronic condition. He additionally got benefit from overcoming his fear of the stigma of having an evaluation by a psychiatrist for pharmacological intervention. Fortunately, Richard had an excellent response to just a low dose of an anti-depressant medication, which lowered the frequency and the intensity of OCD obsessions and compulsions, giving him a sense of peace.

For Richard, self-empowerment in mental health meant assembling and utilizing an entire coordinated set of internal and external resources, and learning that living with a chronic psychiatric condition in a high quality of life is indeed possible.

Health

Health

The role of the psychotherapist in medical/health issues is an interesting one. Mental health professional's training – whether it's in psychology, counseling, marriage and family therapy, or social work – is always very quick to point out that it is critical that psychotherapists recognize what is called the "scope of practice" of the mental health professional – and never exceed it, especially when it comes to giving "medical advice", which only medical professionals (MDs, ODs, chiropractors, PAs, nurse practitioners, and nurses) should do.

That said, the role of the psychotherapist in medical and health issues is critical. Having a challenging medical condition practically demands having emotional support, especially by way of individual therapy, group support, or both. My main specialization has been in HIV, and much of my practice over the years has included providing psychotherapy for HIV-positive gay men. But my experience also includes people living with asthma, Lupus, cancer, Multiple Sclerosis, Irritable Bowel Syndrome, and Ulcerative Colitis, to name a few. I've learned lots of things can go wrong with the human body, as fascinating and wonderful as these "machines" are, these bodies that we live in, and "borrow" as a home for our soul for this lifetime, until such time as we return the "loan" and let our body return to earth – "ashes to ashes, dust to dust."

So what is self-empowerment and having the life you want when it comes to health? I think there are several important concepts in this:

First is the Absence of Symptoms. Part of "good health" is having a state of being where our functioning is rather unremarkable – everything moves, nothing hurts, nothing looks or feels different from what we think it should.

Short of that, if we do have symptoms that are an indication of a condition, disease, illness – whatever you want to call it – then the next best thing is to *manage* those symptoms so that they either go away and are resolved, or they are managed so that they have minimal impact on our physical, emotional, social, private and professional functioning.

The management of symptoms begins with self-empowerment. It starts with having enough loving regard for yourself that if you recognize that something is not quite right with your how your body feels, looks or functions, you become energized to take action about it. You call your doctor and make an appointment, or if you have the kind of relationship with your doctor where he allows email inquiries directly to him (mine does; this is not unheard of), you can "check in" and he or she can advise you on whether it's something that requires a very short home remedy or if it's something where your doctor wants you to come in for an appointment.

When I work with people regarding health concerns, I always say the most important word in health care is *access*. That means having access to the expertise, medications, diagnostic equipment, knowledge, observational experience, research, and anecdotal evidence that you need to help you get better. When we think of the poor people in Africa who died of AIDS long after effective medications for treatment were available, it was a problem of *access* to medications. When a person faces a certain condition that is beyond the ken of local physicians, you might have to drive or fly to get *access* to a super-specialist who can help you – like Dorothy's journey on the yellow brick road to see the Wizard, in order to have access to his "wisdom" (hopefully most doctors you go to in this situation are not "humbugs" like the Wizard was!). Access also includes *affordability*, which health care reform is helping to address.

Another way of looking at health besides just the absence of symptoms is the presence of the classic indicators of health. When you have these, you're coming awfully close to having the life you want in health. These include having a good appetite, having enough energy to complete the tasks you set for yourself throughout the day – including domestic tasks, professional, and recreational tasks, and having regular systems of breathing comfortably, digesting food comfortably, and having regular urinary and bowel functions. It also includes having a strong libido, and a "lust" for life and playfulness at any age that approximates what very young people have. It includes a comfortable mobility, having all your limbs and joints functioning in a way that you can do any task, strike any pose, and achieve any motor task that humans generally can do. In my work with dancers, acrobats, and other super-humans, sometimes this includes functioning in ways that only a small population can do. And all of this is done in the absence of pain that signals the body a certain move, function, or task is not possible due to some malady of injury, inflammation, abrasion, or dysfunction.

New Age author Louise L. Hay, who soared to fame in the late 1980s, was famous for the concept of loving the self, and its healing effects on the body. Her seminal books, You Can Heal Your Life, and Heal Your Body, espoused the idea that much of disease is about "dis-ease" of the spirit. Her books included a chart that listed many different maladies, and their underlying spiritual cause relating to the sense of self – for example, she related cancer to resentment, giving an inspiring example of herself who faced cancer and claims to have "cured herself" through affirmations and visualization. This is, of course, highly controversial, and occasionally we have seen in various books and articles a "battle" between Eastern and Western philosophies of treating illness. In my observation, I think sometimes the "granola types" who really criticize Western medicine are engaged in some kind of anti-corporate class warfare, where what they're really criticizing is the socially questionable issue of pharmaceutical companies making billions in profit. Unfortunately, some people who refuse medication based on the feeling that pharmaceutical companies are just out to screw them can sometimes end up self-sabotaging their own medical care, exacerbating suffering and even helping to cause their own death. I'm all for social responsibility by global corporations, but at the same time, I don't have a paranoia that all Western medicine is poison to be avoided. I always have said, if Mr. Wrigley can get rich selling chewing gum, then Mr. Abbott (as in Abbott Laboratories, makers of Kaletra, a potently effective anti-HIV medication) can get rich off of saving my life!

But Louise Hay's philosophies have proven extremely valuable to all of her fans, and to me. A positive attitude is critical in the management of any acute or chronic illness. It just helps a person put their best foot forward. Hay's concept that it all begins with Loving the Self is ingenious. Toward the end of her flagship book, You Can Heal Your Life, a poem printed in beautiful calligraphy talks about "I love myself, therefore…" and the phrases include affirmations about taking care of the self, in terms of nutrition, exercise, grooming, and creating a safe, comfortable, aesthetically pleasing home. I teach many clients about this concept, with the idea that if we start many statements with "I love myself, therefore…", we fill in the blanks with plans and directives for ourselves that come from a positive space and lead to good, sound, healthy decisions.

This philosophy helps us to adopt a comprehensive healthy lifestyle, that includes nutrition, exercise, medical care, and the component that way too many people neglect, stress management and emotional self-care. It has been theorized that women generally outlive men because women have faced less stress over their lifetime. We tend to focus on the illnesses themselves, and not on the emotional and social factors that might have contributed to a "climate for illness."

So much of what I help clients with who are facing various physical challenges is what I call "the other half" of health care. Of course, having access to an educated, credentialed, and skillful physician is of paramount importance, especially having access to a specialist. For people with chronic health conditions, you must be treated by someone who has seen this before and knows how to recognize it and treat it with the most up-to-date treatment techniques available that lead to the most positive outcomes – from saving the person's life, to curing them, or at least providing the highest quality of life possible, including in terminal illness providing "palliative" (end-of-life) care. If a malady is not curable, then treatment that aims to improve or sustain quality of life is the next order of business.

If we put the focus in medical treatment on quality of life, we are doing well. Sometimes the patient has to be their own advocate with their doctor, speaking up, for example, if a new medication gives them uncomfortable or even intolerable side-effects, even if they have been ordered to take it. In my experience, far too many doctors see the patient as an organism or a subject, and forget that there is a real person there who has to suffer if a medication gives side-effects. The best doctors respond to the patient's concerns, and mitigate the side-effects with either additional drug prescriptions, "home remedy" recommendations that they have observed work in others in their experience (ginger for nausea, aloe for cuts), or switching them to another drug that is likely to treat the symptoms or disorder. With today's plethora of medications available on the market, and a certain "healthy competition" among pharmaceutical companies, if one drug doesn't work for you, it's likely that another will – perhaps more effectively and with fewer side effects. Again, having ACCESS to this is key in medical management.

Of course, with any medical disorder, "an ounce of prevention is worth a pound of cure." So, how, exactly, does one prevent illness? For this concept, I turn my attention to perhaps an idealized vision of a 19th Century pioneer. Sure, many people in the 19th Century died of disorders that would be cured nearly instantly today, but the active lifestyle of the frontiersman (or woman) provides a certain example of a hale and hearty American lifestyle. Close-to-the-Earth foods, few artificial ingredients, much physical action, community support, clean air and water, and a certain "working with" the physical environment are all examples. Many people would say if your grandmother couldn't pronounce it, or didn't eat it, you shouldn't, either.

I'm not a purist – I admit that one of my favorite after-work rituals is to sit down with a small snack of nacho cheese Doritos and a small glass of caffeine-free Pepsi. I think this is one of my favorite parts of my day. And although nutritionist purists would cringe at such choices, they might rejoice that I might follow that up with a low-carb dinner of lean meat, steamed vegetables, and brown rice. Maybe it's just my Libra personality, but to me, food and fitness are sort of a lesson in balance.

Other examples of food management that work for me include trying to snack on raw fruits and vegetables, which I happen to love, and of course being generally active in terms of fitness. I'm not in fitness-model-perfect shape, but I do OK for being well over 40 and still wearing the same pants size I wore in high school (which I realize doesn't sound that impressive, except when I add I'm a 30 waist/32 inseam; I'm proud of that).

Quite a few clients mention body image or a desire to lose weight in the early stages of therapy. I have strong opinions on this:

First, we have to realize that body size and shape, and what is considered desirable, is culturally bound. A person we might call heavy or overweight today might have been considered just well off or portly a hundred years ago. Actresses in Hollywood, or male fitness models, or Madison Avenue runway fashion models, all would be judged by very harsh standards of physique or figure. These are profession-bound values, and there are movements (mostly women's advocacy) to challenge the idea that the uber-lean people we see in magazines in any way resemble reality.

In Los Angeles, however, they do. Walking around West Hollywood, one would see men who haven't touched a carb in weeks! In this kind of environment, any man who doesn't have six-pack abs would be looked on with suspicion – and that's if he's even looked at at all. It's the culture of some gay men to demand particularly defined physiques of one another. The same holds true for women in media, from weather girls to runway models. We have to remember that our environment can put pressure on us either way – to be obsessively fit, or not – depending on where we live in the country. That kind of influence is not self-empowered; self-empowerment when it comes to weight and body shape is the relationship with our bodies that we develop ourselves, "competing" only with ourselves, and making choices about diet and exercise that are congruent with our values, beliefs, and priorities.

When a client talks to me about weight loss, I quickly reiterate that I am not a personal trainer nor a nutritionist, who are the professionals (along with physicians) you might think would address body weight and shape issues. But I do think there is a role for a psychotherapist in this, and for applying Cognitive Therapy in particular, to understand how the client views himself/herself, what assumptions (positive or negative) they hold about their bodies and appearance, and the nature of their self-esteem.

I worked with a woman who was quite a Cinderella story. She had beautiful hair and eyes, but was probably fifty pounds over the weight her doctor would have recommended. We worked primarily on improving her relationships with co-workers, but as a secondary goal, we looked at her quest for weight loss. Under a doctor's supervision, she enrolled at a nearby gym, and hired a personal trainer for exercise sessions and to provide her with a simple calorie-counting diet. She worked out hard and followed the diet plan, and not only lost the fifty pounds she started with, but ten more. She looked radiant in her new figure – and got a lot of attention for it socially. On a Monday, she came in to therapy philosophical. She related how over the weekend, probably half a dozen men asked to buy her drinks at her favorite local watering hole. She sighed and marveled that she had been going to this same restaurant lounge for years, and never had men ask to buy her drinks. She was frustrated; she was still the same person, she said, just in a different package. I responded that while the world shouldn't work that way, it does, and we need to accept that strangers, anyway, are going to respond to us in a certain way based on how we look. It sounds superficial, but as AA says, "living life on life's terms" means that these things must be considered. But it always starts with self-esteem, and understanding that we are good, whole, worthy people, regardless of any external characteristic. We need to love and accept ourselves first, as we are, then we proceed to make any changes we want (losing weight, Botox, cosmetic procedures, diets, exercise plans, etc.) If we try to say we will love ourselves only when we "look" the way we want, we might not ever get there. Self-empowerment is loving the body we are given, and only making changes carefully, under the supervision of qualified professionals (especially a doctor) and with a mindfulness of what we are doing, and why – with realistic expectations of how we expect our lives to change when something in our appearance changes.

Much has been said about the "mind-body" connection, and when I work with a client on a health-related issue, their therapy is a whole process about the delicate dance between the mind and body. The two are inseparable. Again, Louise Hay's work delineates this, as do other major self-help authors such as Bernie Siegel, MD, in his book, <u>Love, Medicine, and Miracles</u> and Deepak Chopra, among many others. Part of what I think is an individual's coping process with chronic or even acute illness is the journey of exploration of the Self, and self-awareness, to see what works for you. It's a very individual, idiosyncratic process. For some reason, jasmine tea is especially medicinal to me when I'm sick – which I discovered years ago with a bad bout of food poisoning. Part of self-empowerment in health care is eating, drinking, or doing something and then listening with a certain "third ear" to your body, and listening for when your body says, "Yeah, I like that, do that again." Conversely, you can also use this third ear for when your body says, "Eh; not so good; lay off that, will ya?" With time and a little practice, you can develop an entire repertoire of foods, drinks, behaviors, settings, and even rituals that help you to feel better whenever you are in "sick mode."

When I was in the hospital a few years ago for a total hip replacement (yes, at 43; it happens), having a fan brought into the room so there was a constant gentle stream of fresh air blowing on me in the somewhat hot, stuffy room made all the difference. Little comforts when one is acutely ill can really help, and give us a behavioral way of actively coping with our plight. My mom taught me this as a kid, and I can't look at Lipton tea without thinking of how she would bring that to me when I was sick and it always tasted so good. She knew all kinds of little tricks to help things feel better. Being ill is a physical experience, but it has emotional ramifications.

It's important to remember that it is the natural state of the body to want to be healthy and high-functioning. Millions of years of evolution support this. So when you are ill, try to get in tune with the natural healing powers of the body to recognize that this is supposed to be temporary, and "this, too, shall pass."

Challenges: Health

A lack of self-empowerment when it comes to health is as common as air. I really feel sorry for this state, and it has to do with all kinds of cultural influences from government, health insurance, pharmaceuticals, corporations, and very destructive and misleading "folk knowledge" that tends to "get it all wrong" when it comes to health information. There are so many competing industries and stakeholders in health care, that what is best for the patient is obscured politically, socially, culturally, financially, and of course medically.

People are disempowered when it comes to their health when they have symptoms that harm them, yet they don't know what is causing them. They are disempowered when they know what kind of help they need, but they can't access it (it's too far; it's too booked up; it's too expensive; it's too scary; it sounds painful; my friend said it doesn't work, "they" say not to do it, etc.). Self-empowerment in health, therefore, is the reverse of these things. It's understanding what works about your health, and what doesn't. If it doesn't work, self-empowerment is finding out why. Taking care of ourselves in terms of health is an arduous a task. There is much information to process. Add cultural or linguistic barriers for certain populations, and the situation is worse.

Another aspect of self-empowerment in health is resisting what I call just plain bad information. Hearsay. Rumor. Internet chat rooms. Bad science. What Aunt Hilda said. Commercial interests disguised as a science to influence you, when they are really just trying to influence you to open your wallet, without receiving much value for it (the over-use of supplements comes to mind). Self-interest of doctors, practitioners, government agencies trying to save money, health insurance companies trying to cut care to increase profit, and pharmaceutical companies misleading the public about the risks or the value of their products because to tell the whole truth might hurt profits.

Self-empowerment means understanding that these exploitive forces exist, and using our powers of critical thinking to resist their petty influence, and evaluate the information we are presented with, and judge it according to our own research, experience, and even intuition. If you take a medicine that's supposed to "help" you, but you are very sick from taking it, self-empowerment means telling your doctor this and insisting on a different medicine, or at least knowing why it is making you ill and what your options are. Self-empowerment means that you have equal power (if not more so) in a relationship with a doctor, nurse, social worker, pharmacist, physical therapist, technician, etc. – you are hiring them as paid expert consultants; you are not a slave to "doctor's orders." Doctors present choices based on their expert consultation to the patient for them to make an informed, self-empowered evaluation of their options, with monitoring and support as follow-up.

Self-empowerment in health is realizing that we are all entitled to human rights such as food and beverages to nourish us, a decent night's sleep, stable ("euthymic") mood, a good appetite, a good sex drive, mobility of our limbs free from pain, a functioning digestive and elimination system, and a stable and intact body, free of disfigurement or dysfunction. These are our rights, and self-empowerment is keeping the commitment and the courage to ourselves to exercise them. It is understanding that we are all worthy of being "intact" in the above ways, or else we are going to advocate for ourselves to get access to the resources we need to achieve this, no matter how long, or whatever it takes.

Health

Case Study: "Thomas"

My client, Thomas, was a twenty-nine-year-old gay white male who came to me in acute distress due to a recent diagnosis as HIV-positive. Smart, handsome, and extremely conscientious as a junior computer science executive, he was not one to know "vulnerability." He was always smart, he was always physically accomplished as a high school tennis star, and he came from a wealthy East Coast family. So the contrast of being a high-achiever, and yet suddenly feeling scared, disempowered, and helpless was daunting, not only for what those things were by themselves, but for the unpleasantly "new" experience of it all.

Self-empowerment for Thomas was a fairly straightforward task in therapy. He needed to restore the equilibrium and confidence that was always so familiar to him. Working from a strengths-based perspective, I encouraged him to learn all he could about HIV, so that he could dispel myths and understand what it meant – and what it does NOT mean – to be HIV-positive in modern times (mainly, that the relatively rapid illness and death common at the height of the AIDS crisis no longer exists, and yet diligent medical and psychological self-care are still important).

Self-empowerment does indeed come more easily when a person is especially intelligent and can research, identify, "take in", process, and apply information resources easily. Thomas could do just that. He easily identified and got access to a local HIV-specialty physician for his medical care. He began a medication regimen based on a medical assessment of his HIV viral load measurement, and had the behavioral skills to follow that regimen diligently, as HIV medications require strict adherence to maintain therapeutic levels in the blood.

In therapy, I used a cognitive-behavioral approach to challenge some of Thomas's negative beliefs about himself, that being HIV-positive would make him undesirable to his young gay peers, as being the "diseased pariah" no one would want. We challenged this idea by focusing on his strengths, and what he offered to the community. Throwing himself into a regimen of medical, physical, professional, and even grooming self-care, he established and maintained a visage of the consummate gay eligible bachelor, and became popular among his peers, who admired his early professional accomplishments, his hard-won earnings growth, and his commitment to an idealized fitness plan that made him look more like a young actor or fitness model than a computer executive.

Over time, Thomas began to let go of the negative phantom ideas that his life was over due to his diagnosis. He became self-empowered to understand that having a chronic health condition demands the appropriate time and attention to manage it, so that it doesn't worsen, but also to have enough "healthy denial" to not let it take any more of his time or attention than was necessary. Self-empowerment in health means that you are more than your disease!

Relationships and Sex

Relationships and Sex

In my practice, my client's work is often around relationships – mostly romantic/sexual/domestic ones, but also ones with coworkers, family, and platonic friends. Complex relationships are what make us human, and are perhaps the most important aspects of our lives.

I'll address work and community relationships later, but for now, let's look at those romantic/sexual/domestic ones. I mention all three aspects of those because I think at any given time, the conflicts we have with a significant other – or with someone who has the potential to be – are in one of those three areas.

I've said in articles that I believe in the "Six Lights Theory": For relationship compatibility, it's as if we were like computer modems with various "status lights" that light up if the modem is working properly. We have one at our head, where it lights up if the person we are with interests us, and stimulates us intellectually. We have another one at our heart, if the person touches us emotionally and romantically. And we have another one at our crotch, if the person interests and arouses us sexually. In order for a relationship to really work, all three of our lights – plus all three of theirs – have to be lit. If any one of those six lights is dimmed or burned out, there is conflict. Many times in individual therapy that is about addressing a relationship, or in couples therapy, we are working to try to brighten one or more of those lights again.

Much has been written about relationships, and so much of it is complicated and inaccessible to the average reader, especially when we get into the theories of the psychodynamics of relationships, and how our childhood "stuff" gets triggered in our adult domestic relationships. I think psychoanalytic therapists have been of great help to a great number of couples, but when I work on relationship issues, I try to wrap it in language that the average person will understand, so they can apply certain concepts to making changes in their thinking and behavior that will give them a more peaceful, romantic, happy home.

I explain to couples in therapy that there are a number of usable concepts to understand relationship conflict. One of these is the idea that each partner falls on a continuum between two extremes – enmeshment on one end, and estrangement on the other. When the partners of a relationship are enmeshed, they are "entangled", like the mesh of a rope net. Their individuality is obliterated, and they are like conjoined twins, with no validation or opportunity for expressing their uniqueness and individuality. They have lost much of the strength of their identity of who they were before they entered the relationship. It's as if they are not "two joined as one," they are like "two halves forming a whole"; each one is not sustainable without the other. They must do everything together, and there is no room for individual expression. On the other extreme, estrangement, the partners of the couple are too distant, functioning almost like platonic roommates, coming and going so involved in their own careers, hobbies, friends, and other individual pursuits, that they hardly look like a couple. They are just indifferent to one another. All partners naturally fall somewhere on this continuum, and usually we find if one partner is nearer to one extreme, and the other partner is nearer to the other. Then the task in therapy becomes finding a way to meet one another at some compromise point on the continuum to increase intimacy. Or, both partners can be at one end or the other, and the task in their therapy is to move them both toward the middle (unless both partners are quite content at one end or the other).

For example, a couple who is enmeshed and feeling "on top of one another" (in the bad way, that is) might have to deliberately cultivate ways of spending some time apart to explore individual hobbies and interests that their partner does not share. In heterosexual couples, this is often achieved through gender-role interests – the husband might go off and play golf, the wife might join a book club. In gay or lesbian couples, the interests might be less about gender interests, and more just individual hobbies – one might join a bicycling group, while the other joins a bowling club. By taking on these new, separate, individual interests, there is a sense that "absence makes the heart grow fonder", and the members of the couple have new, interesting things to talk about when they both get home from their respective hobbies. There is "elbow room" and "breathing space" brought back into the relationship, and there is a freshness to the relationship, and a paradox that spending more time apart actually brings them closer together.

For a couple who is estranged, they might need to behaviorally address that by planning a weekly "date night" where they go to dinner, a movie, a concert, or something else together. They look for ways to tackle projects together around the house, or plan more vacations (budget allowing). They might double-date with another couple. They put more emphasis on doing things as a two-person family, as a dyad unit.

Another dynamic that couples often attempt to manage in couples therapy is where one partner fundamentally has a fear of engulfment, and another has a fear of abandonment. Fear of engulfment is the fear that the relationship smothers the individual, much as in the dynamics of enmeshment. He (or she) feels that the relationship doesn't allow them to "breathe", and that an important sense of individuality is obliterated by relationship obligations and even the pressure to do everything together. The partner feels that he is not at his best, and that while he might still want his partner, he wants to set some distance or else he feels confined. The inner child gets triggered in conscious or unconscious ways. His approach is like a child with an over-protective parent who yearns to be free to explore the world at his own pace and make his own discoveries. The partner with the fear of abandonment is just the opposite. He or she gets anxious at the idea of separation, even temporary ones. There is a discomfort that is directly proportional to the frequency or duration of absences from their partner. Separation feels like a "bad thing" that is to be minimized for a healthy home. This often has its roots in the partner's childhood, where a traumatic loss (such as the death or neglect of a parent, sibling, or close friend) leaves a sensitivity to a, "No! Don't leave me!" feeling. Even a child who witnessed his parents' divorce can experience this, where even unconsciously in adult life, it becomes, "No! Don't go to the store! You might not ever come back, just like Dad did!" These partners need reassurance that his or her partner is always "there", even if there is time apart. It's learning to trust that what goes away temporarily does not cease to exist; it's merely out of sight for a while, and is coming back – and is always "there" emotionally.

Still another example that is similar to these dynamics in relationships is where one partner is primarily a Distancer, always "escaping" his partner a bit, and the other is the Pursuer, always chasing his partner. If one examines most relationships, one can see how each partner adopts one or the other of these roles. When they are exacerbated is when conflict arises, and conflict resolution lies in adopting empathy for the other person's role, and adjusting more to the other role in ways that are concrete, behavioral manifestations.

Most of us "need" or want relationships, but even when we are partnered or married, we still need to balance "alone time" versus "together time." In our busy, modern lives, where we are working more hours than ever due to modern economic pressures, we only have so much time out of the office to work with. With this free time, we have to attend to all domestic chores and responsibilities, and what's left of truly free time must be balanced between time to ourselves, which is necessary for mental health, and time with our significant other, extended family, and perhaps children.

Relationship conflicts don't get resolved until both partners are open and "game" to the idea of experimenting with changing something about their thinking, seeing things from a different point of view, and making at least some changes in their behavior. This usually comes about as a result of awareness, which comes through communication, and then making a commitment to at least experiment with getting out of the old ruts of behavior and trying something new. It's also about each partner making a REQUEST of the other, in concrete behavioral terms: "OK; I'll commit to taking the trash out more often, if you commit to putting the cap back on the toothpaste." Or, "I'll try to be more affectionate, if you try to stop criticizing me for small things."

Sex and Couples Therapy

This kind of communication and compromise applies not only to resolving disputes about domestic life such as household chores, but in the bedroom as well. Having a good sex life in a relationship is an ongoing challenge, a living, breathing entity that is like a garden that needs to be tended to in order to be green, colorful, and thriving. An unattended garden eventually will wither if it's not watered, fertilized, and able to get sufficient sun and nutrients. Having a good sex life is a process, not an event. You don't just "arrive" at it, it must evolve over time according to the needs of each partner. Dr. Ruth Westheimer, the diminutive and ubiquitous sex expert of the 80s, was big on couple's communication during sex, and emphasizing that the brain is the primary sex organ. Much of what I do in couples therapy regarding sexual issues is what I call "sexual troubleshooting", where we identify conflicts or dissatisfactions on behalf of one partner, or both, regarding the frequency, type, and duration of sex. Troubleshooting sexual issues in a couple very often becomes a collaboration between psychological dynamics of the therapy room, and physical/medical issues that need to be addressed by a gynecologist or urologist. There can be problems with overall desire, problems with sexual function (such as erectile dysfunction), or problems with satisfaction with what's being done or not done in the bedroom. There is also the interplay of the couple's emotional dynamics and sex life. I have worked with couples on simply the emotional issues, such as resolving conscious or unconscious conflict, and miraculously the sexual complaints identified early in treatment and not addressed since are resolved – merely by resolving the emotional conflicts first. One challenge in couples therapy is knowing when sexual issues can be addressed in standard couples counseling, and when a referral to a specifically trained sex therapist is in order.

I'm always a little leery about therapist bias in couple's issues. I hear horror stories with alarming frequency from some clients who come to my office and relate experiences from previous therapists' behavior that is clearly unethical or even illegal. Therapist neutrality in couples work is an ongoing challenge, because despite our best efforts, it's only human to somehow side with one partner versus another, and lose objectivity. However, when a therapist sees a couple, their "client" is not one partner, nor the other, nor even both partners – the client in couples therapy is the entity of the relationship that lies between them. It is the health of this entity that the therapist is trying to support. And yet, if the therapist is mired in his or her own biases when it comes to the issues the partners present, they can be hampered in their effectiveness.

For example, if a therapist is a member of AA, and they see a couple where one partner has a drug or alcohol issue, there can be an enormous temptation to make the drinker/user the "offender" who needs to literally "get with the program" – ignoring perhaps the role of the other partner in contributing to the conflict. If the therapist is very socially conservative, and sees a heterosexual couple where one partner is thinking of leaving the relationship due to "coming out", there might be a bias to label the gay or bisexual the "guilty" party, rather than helping the couple understand the nature of sexual orientation/identity, and how to address this in the couple.

Every partner in couples therapy should at least consider at different points in their therapy whether they feel there is a bias on the part of the therapist that the partner needs to bring up in session and address. It is *much* better to bring up any concerns about the therapist *to* the therapist, rather than merely dropping out of treatment with no explanation to the therapist on why his clients took a powder in the middle of treatment. This sort of interaction with a therapist often opens valuable avenues for discussion and actually *helps* the therapeutic process. Also, it gives your therapist a chance to address his or her mistakes – it's therapeutic for you, and good feedback to the therapist to help them address their blind spots and biases to make them a better service provider to you and the community.

But when couples therapy is good, it's really good. Couples therapy can reignite the passions of a relationship and turn partners who are frustrated and unhappy into ones that are playful, romantic, and optimistic. This is a really rewarding thing for a therapist to witness, and is one of the reasons I enjoy working with couples. As the AA saying says, "It works, if you work it" – that's true of couples therapy, too.

Much of the work in couples therapy is about building the Skills of Relationship, which is not a subject taught in school, but is critical for happy adult living (unless you are single, which is another topic). The only down side to doing couples work as a therapist that I find is that it is somewhat repetitious – couples dynamics tend to be awfully similar from one couple to the next, regardless of their background. This is true for straight, gay, and lesbian couples —we don't even get much diversity of dynamics there. Because so often the idea of Having the Life You Want when it comes to relationships is mastering the three main skills of relationship, what I call the "Three C's"– Commitment, Communication, and Compromise.

The cute alliteration of those elements is merely coincidental, but it does make it easier to remember. Without a basic commitment to the relationship, you have no foundation to work with. To manage the day-to-day stressors of a relationship, and to keep a relationship strong over theoretically many decades, there simply must be a basic commitment to the idea that, hey, we are in this together. We are doing this. We are making this work. We are in this for the long haul. Separation is not an option. How "adult" this is; as opposed to a very immature philosophy that relationships are "easy come, easy go." Commitment can be symbolized by the act of getting married, for those who are legally able to do so (which same-sex couples are denied in many states), but commitment can also be symbolized by moving in together, or for couples who for whatever reason do not want to move in together, commitment can be ritualized in some other way. But each couple should have some sort of moment, even just a serious conversation, where they are consciously saying, OK, from this day forward, we are making a commitment to support each other and view each other as a two-person family, a dyad, a unit. It's a thing of consciousness. Wearing rings, for example, is an outward symbol of this commitment, and helps to keep each member of the relationship focused.

If you approach all conflicts in the relationship with an attitude of, "No one is leaving, no one is going anywhere, we are safe here, but we are going to work through this," it's much safer. As many authors have said before, no one should threaten to leave a relationship until their bags are packed and sitting at the door. Triggering abandonment in your partner before this point is cruelty (which is another "c", but one that should be avoided in relationships!)

Conflict in relationships (yet another "C") occurs at times when the commitment to the relationship is undermined. Serious flirtations or affairs, for example, undermine the commitment to the primary partner. Drugs, alcohol, or behavioral addictions, also can undermine the basic commitment in a relationship, because that is putting something (as opposed to someone) ahead of your primary partner.

Communication as the next major skill in relationships is also mandatory. Without communication, you have no tool to foster the exchange of information that is necessary for understanding one another. You must be able to accurately send and receive messages in order for a sense of empathy to be built between the two of you. The whole "Imago" relationship therapy model, which is so popular today and developed by Harville Hendrix, Ph.D., author of the great books, Getting the Love You Want and Keeping the Love You Find, among others, emphasizes the basic ability of couples to send and receive messages accurately as a means of resolving conflict and developing intimacy.

The last of these "C's", compromise, is perhaps the most important. Compromise is really the solution to most conflicts. It's about resolving the gulf between two points of view by agreeing to give up a little something in order to get something. And when both partners do this, the gulf of conflict is resolved and you can get on with "the good stuff" in a relationship. Much of compromise is about the dynamic (often performed in couples therapy) of saying, "OK, I'll do this if you do that." The elements that you give up, and the elements that you get, must be of comparable magnitude. It can't be wildly imbalanced, such as, "I'll trim my nails if you sell your motorcycle" (For most motorcyclists, you have to understand asking for that is a request of nearly impossible magnitude). And sometimes you need a couples therapist to be the arbiter of what comparable compromises are. The process of asking for concessions, and getting them, from your partner, tends to build intimacy. It shows you on an unconscious level that your partner is listening to you, and responding to the things that you are trying to convey that are important to you. It's much like the TV show, "Jeopardy!", where the rule is you have to answer the question in the form of a question. In relationships, make your approach to compromise in the form of a request that your partner can accommodate in concrete, behavioral terms. It's not, "I'd like you to be more romantic with me"; it's, "I would really love it if you brought me my favorite flowers, yellow roses, once a month with a card that you wrote yourself." It's not, "I'd like you to be more experimental in the bedroom"; it's, "I want you to take your old silk ties and tie me up tonight and have your way with me." You see the difference? Give your partner something to work with. Again, much of resolving relationship conflict is about making concrete changes in the way you think or behave, from this day forward.

In addition to the "Three C's" of relationship skills, I also work with couples on a concept that I borrow liberally from a couples therapy expert at UCLA, Walter Brackelmans, MD, who is always a popular presenter at the annual "Review of Psychiatry" conference. Dr. Brackelmans laments that "there are too many marriages, and too many divorces" in our country today. And he emphasizes that the core elements of a relationship for him include not "C'"s, but "T's" – the three T's of Time, Talking (and Listening), and Touch (even casual, affectionate, non-sexual touch). In assessing a couple on a first session, I ask to what degree these three T's are being addressed in their relationship. Often, in discussion, we discover that one or more of these T's needs some serious remedial attention. And when the couple identifies ways to increase the under-developed T, whichever one it is, they experience an increased sense of intimacy. Couples need Time together, just to enjoy life doing the recreational things they indulge outside of their working life. Long-term couples, near the end of their lives (my grandparents enjoyed marriages of over sixty-five years apiece), have a sense of time spent together, the times of their lives. Talking and listening is something a couple has throughout their life together, exploring what it means to communicate with someone on everything from the mundane, to the profound, to the intimate. Just think of the many ways you might talk to a partner. It's everything from, "What time is it?", to "What do we do now?" (during a crisis, perhaps), to "dirty" talk in the bedroom. Spending time listening to your partner is perhaps the greatest gift you can give. Touch is a critical element that too often gets ignored. Couples should always kiss goodbye in the mornings, kiss hello in the evenings, and find ways to spontaneously touch through the week. I think this particular practice is one of the subtle things that differentiates truly happy couples from so-so ones. (Never pass your partner in the kitchen while he or she is stirring the pot on the stove while making tonight's dinner without pinching his/her ass as you go by!)

I would add another critical element to the skills of relationship that I talk a lot about with my couples in therapy, and this one overlays the rest, and that is the word REGARD. When you have a sense of regard for your partner, it evokes in you an emotional maturity and discipline to "carry" a relationship that separates an immature, Peter

Pan-like youngster from a mature adult capable of serious emotional long-term bonding with another person. One of my favorite people in the world, Casey Truffo, MFT, who is a business coach for therapists (yes, there are such things), related a story that typifies regard. She went to a fortieth anniversary party of a heterosexual couple she knew. Someone asked the wife what the secret to a long, happy marriage was. The woman answered, "When I get up to pee in the middle of the night, I put the covers back over his shoulders. And when I come back, we hold hands in bed." That, my friends, is regard. Please make a note of it.

Relationships of all kinds are subject to subtle dynamics and unseen forces that guide and even rule relationships, outside of our consciousness. I have worked with couples by asking them what is "written" in what I call the "Unwritten Rule Book" of your relationship. These are customs, traditions, habits and practices that both partners collude in following, and yet they might never have been openly discussed – it just turns out that way. For example, does one of you always choose what restaurant you go to? What movie you see? How you spend free time? Who you spend time with? What topics are, or are not, discussed in your home? So, who wrote those rules??

Sometimes in couples therapy we need to examine what is on page 42, paragraph 3, line 6 of the Unwritten Rule Book, then get out our erasers, rub it out, and re-write the line to better serve the partners in the relationship as it stands now. Making the unconscious conscious is one way of uncovering maladaptive dynamics in the relationship that are bringing you down.

Couples always operate not in a vacuum, but in the context of a social, historical, cultural, and familial context. Each partner of a couple is influenced by being situated in a Family of Origin, meaning your relatives by blood, adoption, or marriage, and your Family of Choice, who are the people you surround yourself with who are close to you by way of relationships you've chosen to develop over time. These can be your friends, neighbors, and colleagues. For couples to thrive, they need support from both of these sources. I would also add the importance of receiving support from society and the law; gay and lesbian couples know all too well how societal or legal lack of support (such as being denied the options of civil marriage or adoption/fostering children) can negatively affect them. The "person in environment" theory that I was taught in my graduate studies in social work posits that we all function in relation to the world and environment around us, in an interplay. Couples are the same way. Ideally, the surrounding environment in which a couple functions is supportive and enhances the health and well-being of the couple as a unit. If not, this is a troubleshooting of its own that the partners need to address, and intervene until they feel comfortable with the context in which they conduct their relationship.

But romantic/sexual/domestic relationships are not the only ones in our lives. To Have the Life You Want, you need other relationships as well. If you're single, these kinds of relationships are emphasized even more. We all need to have friendships with people whom we identify with. Some of the tenets of Self Psychology, popularized by Heinz Kohut, include the concept that we need to see ourselves "mirrored" in other people in order to have a sense of well-being and optimal mental health. Often, these friends can be our peers who are very similar demographically – they can be similar to us in gender, age, race, income, culture, sexual orientation, religion, geographic origin, interests/hobbies, and other variables. Or, they can be quite different from us, and yet some element bonds us together, united in a common interest, avocation, or cause. This is part of the person-in-environment theory, and part of the "no one is an island" concept. Humans are social animals; we exist really only in the context of others.

Relationships with our work colleagues, neighbors, and other members of our community round out our "relationship to relationships." Sometimes the work of individual therapy is troubleshooting conflicts that arise in these kinds of relationships, or sometimes the work is about cultivating these kinds of relationships in the first place, to prevent a sense of isolation and boredom.

Many authors and theorists have discussed how humans, as "social animals", need the contact of others for optimum mental health. Various mental health disorders can disrupt our ability to have optimal social relationships. For example, clients I work with who suffer from Major Depressive Disorder (clinical depression) can self-isolate, which in many ways makes the situation worse. I also work with a number of people with Social Anxiety, which is a socially inhibiting disorder based on an irrational fear of being negatively evaluated by others in social settings (such as a party). Interestingly, the same medications prescribed for Depression can also be prescribed for Social Anxiety, in the "SSRI" (Selective Serotonin Reuptake Inhibitors) family of anti-depressants, and these can work remarkably well in helping someone restore their ability to "get out there" with others.

Beyond our individual psychology, we also need social, interactive relationships to function as a society – at work, in our neighborhoods, in clubs/organizations, and more and more even in our "global community", brought together by international travel and of course the Internet.

In work settings, human relationships make the difference for an enterprise that emphasizes work concepts such as "team players", "esprit de corps", "group effort", and "team spirit." Management will often encourage much of this, because when an organization's employees get along well and work to support one another, productivity (and profitability!) goes up. This is one reason why anti-discrimination laws are so important in the workplace, because the administration is setting a tone that there is an expectation that employees will put individual differences aside for the greater good of doing their job under one roof, with one primary focus for the good of the company.

In neighborhoods, we need cooperation in order to support the domestic tranquility of our individual homes. Anyone who has ever lived in a community group setting such as an apartment or condominium complex knows the importance of the group approaching all matters with patience, respect, and compromise to meet the needs of often very divergent groups of people. A single individual who is somehow causing a disruption can upset the whole atmosphere of an entire complex, for example.

The military is perhaps the strongest example of how human relationships must interact precisely, with its rigid structure of rank, role, and behavior. One could say that the bigger the "mission" of the group, the more "group cohesion" is important.

Other community relationships we find ourselves in throughout our life span feed our need for identification, pride, and celebration of culture. In almost any city, across the year, we find celebrations and observations of community and culture. There are Gay Pride festivals in the summer across the country, Italian-American festivals, religious observances, and cultural/nationality/religious combinations, like St. Patrick's Day. In Abraham Maslow's hierarchy of needs, from the most primitive to the most esoteric, we need to have a sense of community and identity, and celebrate this ritualistically, in order to celebrate who we are, which gives us a sense of being. Even if we aren't necessarily a part of the community which is celebrating something, we can still partake, in a sign of support and celebration – such as celebrating St. Patrick's Day by wearing green, even if we aren't Irish. Having the life you want sometimes means celebrating just because it's there!

Much of our ability to operate socially has to do with how we were raised. Books such as Robert Fulghum's <u>Everything I Need to Know I Learned in Kindergarten</u> illustrate how we need to learn concepts like sharing and getting along. While we need to assert our individual needs in life (or else we sacrifice too much and become co-dependent), if we assert our individual needs (and often just individual "desires") too much, we become boorish and burdensome on others, and come off as arrogant, narcissistic, and self-absorbed—not the best personality qualities for children or adults. Sometimes, the work of psychotherapy is to raise our awareness of where we fall on this precarious spectrum, and make cognitive and behavioral efforts to move ourselves along the spectrum between self-sacrifice and self-indulgence as the need dictates for us to have optimal interactive, human social relationships.

Challenges: Relationships and Sex

Self-empowerment in relationships has many opposites. While many relationships serve their purpose of being profound, mutually beneficial companionship arrangements that enhance life, plenty of relationships exist that embody a lack of self-empowerment.

Relationship members who "cheat" on their partner by breaking a solemn agreement for sexual monogamy undermine the primacy of a relationship. This is why, for some couples, self-empowerment means choosing an alternative to a genital fidelity agreement, and put the emphasis on a romantic/emotional fidelity instead, in an "open" sexual relationship. This is not for all, but for some couples, this model represents equality and honesty. But this is only after a thorough, usually professionally aided negotiation discussion as to the terms of the relationship that protect emotional safety for each partner. It is not self-empowered to simply keep secrets and digress from a primary relationship to have sexual, romantic, or emotional affairs that undermine the dignity of a relationship.

Similarly, it is not self-empowered to be in a relationship where abuse exists. That's not a profound, mutually beneficial arrangement. That is a situation of mind-control, and narcissistic self-indulgence on the part of the abusing partner. It is also gross indulgence of poorly regulated aggressive impulses, usually the result of unresolved trauma of being an earlier victim of abuse themselves and "acting out" in an unconscious compulsion to repeat what was perpetrated on them. Whatever it is, it's not fair to the victimized partner. Self-empowerment when it comes to abusive relationships is reversing the downward spiral of a failing self-perception. It's also about restoring a strong sense of self, and understanding the *inherent* rights of human dignity. Ultimately, self-empowerment in an abusive relationship is finding the courage and support to leave it in a safe way (as opposed to unsafe way, which happens). Self-empowerment in abusive relationships means "getting connected" to organizations and resources that help the abused partner to see the situation for what it is, and not try to save something beyond saving. Abusive relationships are a criminal situation of interpersonal violence, and must be treated as such with both legal and psychosocial support measures.

Perhaps a more subtle example of not being self-empowered in a relationship is just not being happy, and wanting out. This is not an invalid feeling; it happens. Sometimes relationships end with a whimper, and not a bang, and being self-empowered means that perhaps you work on a relationship via a resource such as books or, more importantly, couples counseling, and sometimes you just plain leave. As a self-empowered adult in control of your existential circumstances, sometimes this is necessary, and sometimes it's difficult to explain why. You still have the right to leave; it's your duty to yourself as self-empowered adult to stay if you want to stay, and go if you want to go – for any reason.

Finally, couples need to feel self-empowered to receive the support they need via couples therapy. Couples therapy can and will save many relationships that were headed for a breakup. The scientific, systematic, and clinical validity of the appropriate application of interventions delivered by a competent couples therapist in session can help a couple maintain and enhance their relationship for its duration – not in all cases, especially ones where a basic commitment just isn't there – but in many cases (most, I would say). Being self-empowered means that you bravely avail yourself of such services, and let yourselves be helped by the process.

Sex

I always tell my clients that I believe the most important approach we can take to sex as adults is to employ "sexual self-empowerment", which is saying yes when we want to say yes, without guilt, fear, shame or embarrassment, and saying no when we want to say no, also without guilt, fear, shame or embarrassment. Very early in my career, I ran a 10-session structured support/therapy group for adult male incest survivors. They taught me a lot about their experience, and how sad and vicious sexual abuse/incest can be. One of the worst parts of this kind of abuse is that it can undermine a young person's sense of dominion over his or her own body. We control our bodies – what we ingest, how and where we move it, how we interact with the world around us, and how we interact with the people around us.

When we don't control our own bodies – and when, with whom, and how we interact with others sexually – that is sexual abuse. Sexual abuse is perhaps THE most difficult issue seen in psychotherapy. There is much confusion about this topic, as well as, about whether ALL younger-older sexual relationships are harmful, which was challenged by Judith Levine in her courageous book, <u>Harmful to Minors</u>. The notion that same-sex sexual abuse is "homosexuality" or that it "causes" homosexual orientation is nothing less than profoundly infuriating to those who know the facts to be different. The psychological effects of sexual abuse/incest are very significant and far-reaching. While recovery and healing as a survivor are possible, especially through a combination of individual and group therapy, it takes work, patience, and time. Resources such as books like <u>The Courage to Heal</u> by Ellen Bass and <u>Victims No Longer</u> by Mike Lew are some of my favorites. This topic deserves its own discussion, beyond the scope of this book, but the reader who is a survivor, or loves one, is encouraged to seek out information and support. When I talk about sex, I am assuming we are discussing acts shared between legally consenting adults, or legal "Romeo and Juliet" teens who are sexually active but both legally underage.

My approach to the discussion of sex in therapy is very "sex-positive"; I challenge many clients' notions (usually based in being raised in very sex-negative religions and traditions in the history of America with the Puritans) that sex is "bad", "dirty", "wrong", "secret", "sick", "perverted", "sinful", etc. Being sex positive also includes being LGBT- (lesbian, gay, bisexual, transgender) affirmative, and kink-affirmative (bondage/discipline, or sado-masochism play). Things like BDSM are often actually quite intimate experiences, among trusting, attentive, communicative, consenting adults in safe, sane, and consensual fantasy "scene" play. It is not to be misconstrued with abuse, incest, rape, violence, or a repetition compulsion (re-enacting childhood abuse as a means to come to terms with the abuse). As adults, we have dominion over our own body, and we can indulge its desires, lusts, longings, stimulations, and passions with other consenting adults in appropriate settings to satisfy our very natural inclinations, which is part of what makes us human. We can also have dominion over our bodies to say no. We can say no to anything that makes us feel unwanted pain (emotional or physical), awkwardness, shame, humiliation, or even inconvenience – or, anything that is outside our values, priorities, and goals, which can include social or spiritual/religious considerations. But I challenge clients who have internalized negative messages about sex from the religion of their family of origin, in a way that leaves them feeling sexually dis-empowered from what they want and need naturally (this is especially true of LGBT persons, but other populations can be made to feel "bad" or "wrong" about their sexuality, such as women, people of color, people with physical or mental disabilities, or even people whom many might call "unattractive." We all need love, folks, not just the Pretty People with idealized bodies and magazine-spread looks). Being sexually self-empowered means that we apply critical thinking to the ideas we were brought up with about sex, and we keep the ones that we feel are right for us, in our values as independent adults, and we discard the ones that no longer serve us in our adult identity, or the ones that make us feel bad about ourselves and the glorious Miracle Machine that is our body.

There is much said these days about "sexual addiction." I have colleagues who make a fortune playing into this. I'm not so sure whether the condition is that prevalent, or that there are a lot of very sexually dis-empowered people out there who are acting out of a sexual guilt into dysfunctional behaviors that manifest sexual non-empowerment, such as doing sexual acts that are not congruent with the activities, times, places, and people ideally they would be. "Sex addiction" is quite controversial in that it is NOT currently a diagnosis in the Diagnostic and Statistical Manual of Mental Disorders IV-TR (American Psychiatric Association), and a number of sexologists challenge the very coining of sex as an "addiction" when it is a perfectly natural human process. What is "appropriate" sex can vary greatly by time, place, and culture in history. Some of the activities that were quite common in Western culture during the 1960s and 1970s would likely be labeled as "sex addiction" or "acting out" today. The old joke goes, "A slut is someone who has sex one more time per year than you do."

I frankly think too many psychotherapists are making way too much money on "treatment" and "treatment centers" for "sex addicts", when many times the people facing such programs do not need to be told they are "bad", "wrong", "addicts", "home-breakers", "philanderers", "sluts", etc., when they really need support and validation for a healthy sexual expression and actually a BUILDING of their self-esteem and a positive sense of self. I have treated some people who certainly had sex-addiction-like problems, but I have often found that instead of needing to be confronted for their "bad" behavior, or that they must go to Twelve Step meetings so they can learn about their "character defects" that make them "act out", they really need help building their positive self-esteem and developing a Sexual Sobriety Plan that not only includes eradicating the "bad" (that word again) behaviors they want to stop, that they find exhausting or demoralizing, but also identifying and exalting the "good" sexual behaviors they want to use to express their natural sexuality in ways that leave them feeling supported, refreshed, excited, and relieved, and not humiliated or shamed, all in a context of the people, places, and situations they deem right FOR THEM.

I'm also not one of those people who labels pornography as "all bad, all the time, for all people, in all situations, always", the way we find shockingly frequently in society. Using porn as a sexual enhancement, and not as a burden or drain on one's quality of life, is a delicate balance. Nowhere is this battle as pronounced as between heterosexual men and women. Women misunderstand the degree to which men are visually stimulated in sex, and that viewing porn does not mean that men love their wives or girlfriends less. Some complain that "if you really loved me, you wouldn't need porn." That is not sexually self-empowered, because it's failing to understand the basic nature of men's versus women's sexuality and what I call their "sexual arousal systems", which can be grouped together in various ways (gay/straight/bi, male/female, and their variations), but also can be quite idiosyncratic (specific to an individual). I think sometimes human sexuality is about as diverse as our fingerprints in terms of exactly what "turns us on" and how.

Of course, many in our country automatically label any form of same-sex activity between adults as a "sick/bad/wrong/sinful," as well as mislabeling it as a "choice," which is a failure to understand the natural development of human sexual orientation, regardless of antipathy from cultural, or more frequently, religious sources. Even the field of psychotherapy has been used to persecute LGBT people, mostly in a very discredited past, but annoyingly present today in the unethical, ineffective, and emotionally harmful "change" therapies, which claim to be based in psychological "science" but in reality are based in religious bigotry and notions of inherent heterosexist superiority. Much damage to the mental health and well-being of many, many beautiful human beings has been perpetrated by these selfish and hateful notions. Fortunately, in gay-affirmative psychotherapy practiced by mainstream and well-educated therapists across the world, people who have been harmed by prejudices in their past can embrace healing, pride, and joy in themselves, their lives, and their community.

Being sexually self-empowered means that we develop a relationship to our body and our ability to respond to our body's needs, just as it has needs regarding food, water, temperature regulation, rest, stimulation, and closeness to others. When we love ourselves, we take care of our own bodies as adults with the same loving care that our primary caregivers (usually our mothers, but not always) gave us when we were infants. Sex is just one more way we provide for our bodies for our own needs, in ways that are emotionally, physically, culturally, socially, and perhaps even spiritually fulfilling.

Relationships and Sex

Case Study: "Jeanette and Rich"

"Jeanette" was endlessly fascinating, and a lovely vision of the Greek Ideal as a middle-aged woman of about fifty. Most of our work was about Jeanette's recovering her sense of self after ending a long relationship with "Rich", who was the sexy Bad Boy who, for a time, drove Jeanette wild with desire and the excitement of fast driving and fast living. Unfortunately, he also became relentlessly verbally abusive and drove Jeanette's self-esteem into the ground.

When Rich became brazen in his affections for another woman, Jeanette put up with it for a time, but she knew she was becoming less and less self-empowered. She basically tolerated her long-time live-in boyfriend openly having a long-term affair, but was so emotionally (not physically) "beaten down" that she lost the nerve to do what others thought would be obvious: leave the guy!

Fortunately for Jeanette, her lifelong artistic ability manifested itself in a favor to a friend to redecorate her house. Doing it just as a favor for fun, Jeanette's freakish talent and natural skill in interior design was spectacular. She wrote a popular book about interior design, and her clever prose and graphics attracted hundreds of fans quickly – and additional clients.

With an infusion of self-esteem derived from a Midlife Renaissance in a new profession, she became self-empowered by the adulation and income that was unprecedented. Validated by her new life "9 to 5", she was able to re-evaluate what was happening after 5:00 p.m. and kicked the bastard out.

The irony was that the "other woman" was a former good friend, and the two actually maintained a strained but still fairly consistent social relationship, and eventually bonded over their gripes about Rich. But as Jeanette said, "It's so much easier to hear about his antics when it's just not my problem anymore."

With her new-found freedom and success, Jeanette was able to afford a few reasonable cosmetic procedures that made her already patrician beauty even better, and she became truly sexy and vivacious well into middle age, stopping traffic like women 30 years younger. Jeanette got a kick out of this, standing stereotypes about middle-aged women on their ear.

She still likes Bad Boys who drive too fast and smoke too much. But this time, she has set the bar high, and only the men who behave themselves and truly deserve the red-hot cougar get her attention. That's self-empowerment in relationships for our times

.

Career

Career

Having the Life You Want means deriving satisfaction from your life's work. Everyone on earth, even the independently wealthy, do some sort of work, even volunteer work, because it's just part of the human existence. In my work with clients, many of whom are working-age, middle-class people, their "work on work in therapy" is very often the bulk of their treatment agenda.

Work can be for some synonymous with a daily burden, and something they would rather not think about. I disagree with this; I think having the life you want includes being brave, smart, and tireless enough to make plans, efforts, and actions to arrange your life so that you are doing work that you truly love to do, and earning a good income.

I support my clients' efforts in taking control of their work lives not because I'm trying to support the capitalistic system, but because I'm supporting my clients' psychological self-actualization. We need to have work from an existential point of view in order to have a sense of purpose in life. Without this, the risk for depression and low self-esteem is high. Much of our existential sense of purpose is derived from the work we do; "I work; therefore I am." We can point to something and say, "That is my effort. I'm proud of that. I did that." Studs Terkel's famous book, Working, examined the lives of everyday Americans, and put forth the idea that everyone's work contribution means something, and that there is really no such as thing as "small jobs." Even little kids, when they do an art project in preschool or kindergarten and bring it home to say, "Look what I made!" are starting to understand the self-esteem that comes from producing something of your own efforts.

Work also provides structure. Our work can be a predictable, reliable, secure set of operations that helps to guide our daily and yearly lives. This must be balanced, however, with the variety of thoughts, feelings, and experiences that people need to stay "fresh." Humans are very smart animals, and we need varying stimulation and breaks from routines or our brains get frustrated. Without this frustration, we never would have evolved with new inventions and new ways of doing things. Some say, "Discontent is the mother of invention." We need to know that our jobs are going to be there for us, and that the abundance the Universe provides for us daily meets our needs for food, clothing, shelter, protection from the elements, and well-being.

As discussed in the last chapter, work is also about being a part of a community. In our capitalistic society, which at this point is really global, there is a societal expectation that we take care of ourselves, and that each person is expected to work up to his or her individual ability. It is a reasonable expectation. Since humans are interactive, we must each work in our own way, using our unique gifts, talents, and aptitudes, and trust that when others work in theirs, everything will be taken care of.

These concepts seem great when we first examine them. However, when something gets in the way of these ideal sets of circumstances is when disruption to our social and mental health can occur. People find themselves working in jobs they hate. People lose jobs they love, due to corporate takeovers, relocations, or downturns in our collective, mutually reliant economic system that result in layoffs or plant closures. People can become mentally or physically disabled in a way that prevents them from fulfilling the often daunting requirements of working a full-time or even part-time job. It is when things such as these occur that therapy is a supportive resource to evoke adaptive coping and rehabilitation.

The Americans with Disabilities Act was signed into law by the first President Bush. This was signed with bipartisan support due to the knowledge that disabilities occur in any society, through no fault of the person who becomes disabled. Given that human diversity in our population includes people who do not have optimal physical and mental functioning, the ADA was designed to help everyone make the fullest contribution they can, especially with a "reasonable accommodation" on the part of the employer – whether it wants to or not. (Sometimes, people and organizations have to be forced by law to do the right thing). This is an example of a piece of political legislation that actually has enormous implications for the mental health of millions of individuals. I'm surprised at how often I quote the story of how the ADA was developed with my clients in sessions. The reason I do this is because I'm trying to help the client feel empowered, and to understand that just because he or she has some sort of "disability" (or what we might call "differently abled skills"), he or she can still make a meaningful contribution to society, and earn at least a partial income. There are very few people, in my many years of clinical experience, who cannot do SOME sort of work – because humans are THAT diverse. Now, I've worked with many people who receive public benefits from the state or federal government, and are labeled as "totally disabled" for their basic income purposes, but in reality there is still "work" to be done for them to give them a sense of daily purpose, contribution, and reward (such as hobbies, arts, community or volunteer work).

The existential value of work has implications not only for today, but for all time. Part of the existential meaning of our lives is about considering how the work that we do today will affect generations to come. I marvel when I see old-fashioned pictures of the (often Irish) workers who built the New York City skyscrapers in the early 20th Century. They are probably all long since deceased, but their legacy lives on in the work they did. Various famous photographs show them with lunch boxes sitting on exposed beams hundreds of feet in the air, building landmarks that are now part of our iconic American consciousness, like the Empire State Building. (Later, on September 11, 2001, the tragic terrorist attacks to destroy the two World Trade Center towers had so much meaning, killing thousands, terrorizing millions, and destroying in minutes what it took hundreds of brave high-risk workers years to build in preparation for their opening in 1976). But even if we aren't building something that will hopefully stand for generations to come, our daily work is contributing to the future people of the earth. Our psychological well-being and sense of self have their roots in what we do for work, and a sense that we are inter-connected through our daily efforts to run the world.

The work of psychotherapy in regard to work is often about identifying a client's view and vision of his long-term, ideal Professional Self, and working to create that vision into a reality. Sometimes it's about deliberately developing a short-term, medium-term, and long-term career progression plan. Other times it's about planning how to get school or training for effecting a career transition, with planning the rites-of-passage, benchmarks, milestones, and timelines needed. Often, it's about developing a plan for receiving mentoring, networking, and social promotion to achieve a certain status or position (this can be the case for my clients working in the arts in Hollywood, where it's "not what you know, but who you know"). This becomes especially challenging for people who are natural introverts, or who suffer from Depression or Social Anxiety. But for most adults, having the life you want is in many ways having the WORK you want.

Finding the work you want can be a function of coaching/therapy and other supportive professional services. There are various forms of career testing (such as the famous Myers-Briggs), and an exploration of your values, aptitudes, and passions in counseling. These processes can also help you identify the skills, setting, and life purpose for your work. Finding the right career with the aid of counseling requires an investment of time, energy, and money, but is highly rewarding in the evolution of the Professional Self.

Challenges: Career

Unfortunately, at the time of this writing during a lingering recession, self-empowerment when it comes to career is full of deficits for many (some would say most) people. You see it everywhere: people feel "trapped" in jobs they hate, promotions are nearly unheard of, companies are cutting benefits as cost-cutting measures and not restoring them when their profits get better, people have no long-term loyalty to any one company anymore (and rightly so, as the companies demonstrate little to no loyalty to them), and the entire concept of growing your career according to your hopes, dreams, goals, and visions of your Ideal Professional Self takes a back seat to just hunkering down and trying to be grateful that you have a paycheck at all, despite the fact that it hasn't even kept up with inflation.

That said, forget about all that. Because buying into any of those negative forces is no way to achieve self-empowerment in your career. Cognitively, frankly, you need to ignore the recession and focus on three things: 1) The skills you want to use; 2) The setting you want to use them in; and 3) Choosing a worthy audience for your efforts. For example, Ruth could be a nurse (skills), in a private hospital's neo-natal intensive care unit (setting), for the benefit of medically vulnerable premature infants and their families (audience). Mary is a psychotherapist (skills), in a private practice (setting), who specializes in helping single mothers who are raising troubled teens (audience). Mary's friend Jan is a psychotherapist (same skills), but works in a non-profit agency (different setting), for troubled teens and their families (same audience). What are your current skills? What is your current (or desired) setting to use them in? And perhaps most importantly, when you get up for work every morning, who is the audience worthy of your efforts every working day? This is where we, ideally, bring love to our work. We have to somehow love the worthy audience of our efforts, even if it's the motorists who are grateful to us for pumping gas into their cars.

Other pitfalls that I hear often in my practice include dealing with bureaucracy, frustrations with corporate structure, work situations that are demeaning, and the especially unpleasant situation of having a mean boss.

The concept of the "workplace bully" has gotten more discussion in recent years, and a number of the clients I have worked with, in addition to a number of people in my personal life, have experienced this. I have seen instances of near "soul murder" from people who are completely demoralized by unethical, illegal, under-handed, or just overly aggressive behavior from bosses or even peers. Self-empowerment in these situations usually means to cope in the short term, and get out (to another job) in the long term. It also involves exercising your rights, from negotiating a better relationship with the offending person, to reporting the situation to the human resources department of your job. In extreme cases, you might have to consult with an attorney and exercise your legal rights. Since I have worked with many clients who are from cultural or ethnic minorities, or are people with disabilities, they can be the victims of discrimination, and many have won legal settlements for workplace infractions against them. Self-empowerment in these situations means reaching out, getting the expert consultation and support you need, and exercising your rights carefully but also assertively.

There is always the challenge of a need to survive in a commercial world, to provide for yourself, balanced with doing a profession you enjoy. There is also the challenge of which of your various talents and skills are currently held in high esteem in the marketplace. Who will hire us because they find our skills VALUABLE?

People will only part with their money (or their corporation's money on your behalf) if they are convinced that they are getting fair work for what they are paying. There is an old saying, "If you can solve someone's problem, you can find a job." That's true from a corporation who needs a new vice president of global marketing, to a person who's thirsty driving by a lemonade stand. You have to put an ear to the ground and LISTEN for someone who is calling out for the exact kind of help that you happen to have the skills, talent, and willingness to give. Recognize what you do better than most. Approach it from what therapist and business coach Casey Truffo, MFT calls a "how can I serve you?" angle, and you'll find people falling all over themselves to hire you. When someone expresses a need that drives them up the wall, all you need to say (sincerely) is, "Oh, I can help you with that"—and they will open their wallet to pay you practically on the spot.

Self-empowerment in your career can be found in the lyrics of a number of songs that support dreaming, overcoming challenges, and being more than you ever thought possible. Inspired music can be a wonderful tool to energize yourself. Listen for songs that help you to be empowered in what do, or want to do.

Keep working on the development of your Professional Self until you feel that you are bringing a part of yourself, and the love of the labor, every day (OK, except for weekends, holidays, vacations, and retirement – which are all very important), for as long as you live. Bringing love to your work is the ultimate in self-empowerment in your career.

Career

Case Study: "Dean"

My colleague, Dean, was a funny guy. Before I opened my own practice, I was the Clinical Director for a non-profit agency. Dean was the sales/service representative for our photocopiers, and without our photocopiers, our agency would have collapsed! Dean was a generous guy – whenever he made his monthly service call, he would take me out to lunch. He would subtly try to upsell some of the latest equipment or supplies, but mostly it was about keeping us happy as one of his accounts. His stories were great – all about his upbringing, his adventures going surfing on various vacations around the world (Dean sold a LOT of copiers!), and making the most of life. People who make you laugh in life are valuable people to have around.

About a year or so into our monthly lunches, Dean said that the following month, another service rep would be calling on us – permanently. I asked why he was leaving, and Dean explained that he was turning 38 soon. Unfortunately, many members of his family had especially short life spans. He had lost a grandfather, father, and a brother to early deaths from heart disease. Dean was feeling fine, but so had the others up until sudden heart attacks had killed them. So, Dean explained, he was retiring from his work as a photocopier sales/service rep, and moving to Hawaii where he was buying a bread-and-breakfast (again, Dean sold a LOT of copiers!) and opening a surf instruction school – "Teach what you know!" said Dean.

I was sorry to see him go, but I was also very glad for him. How self-empowered, I thought, to take charge of your career, and make the changes you need to have the life you want. In Dean's case, he became empowered to have the life he wanted because of the possibility that his life wasn't very long.

Fortunately, a number of years later, I heard that Dean was very successful with both the bread-and-breakfast and the surf school. Most importantly, he was still alive.

There's an important lesson in this: When it comes to living not only happier, but staying alive – period—reducing stress and taking charge of your career is key.

Finances

Finances

Money. There. I said it. Now, how many people get anxious just hearing the word? For many of my clients, no other word arouses so many emotions.

Just as in the last chapter how I described how work is the foundation for our livelihood for many of us, our relationship to money is significant to our mental health. Our feelings about money are tied to what theorist Abraham Maslow called the "Hierarchy of Needs," where we all need some sort of money to provide for everything from basic items such as food, clothing, and shelter, to higher-order needs such as socialization, entertainment, and a sense of belonging.

Countless books have been written on money – how to make it, how to make more of it, how not to lose it, what it means, what it doesn't mean – and then those books are re-written all over again by new writers for every generation. You can read a book like Think and Grow Rich, by Napoleon Hill, from the 1930s, and it sounds like something that would be on the "new titles" table at the big bookstores today. There have always been social classes, and money has been an issue around the world probably since the Stone Age. And all of these books come down to one message: money is important, but it's not the MOST important; and how you FEEL about money will determine much about your experience with it.

Money is merely the "energy", or tender, behind transactions. I always love the joke Sophia makes in an episode of "The Golden Girls", when she talks about a village in Sicily that used colored rocks for currency, saying that, "To this day, in some villages, two of these [rocks] will get you a veal-and-pepper sandwich." Somehow, when money is reduced to just an object of exchange, it puts it all in perspective.

Several years ago, I wrote a newsletter setting out "Seven Tips for Taking Care of Your Financial Self," and I'd like to share them here with you.

Part of my initial assessment as a psychotherapist examines a client's current financial security, goals, fears, risks, and rewards. Our finances contribute to how we perceive our external environment, and they affect mood, feelings, behavior, and relationships. Over many years in clinical practice, I have observed certain "true-isms" about people who just "have it together" financially – regardless of their income bracket. What is the connection between good financial habits and coping with depression and anxiety? Here are some time-honored tips:

1) **Plan your career** – No other factor I've seen is more important to long-term financial security than your choice of career, and managing that career from the start of your working life until retirement. It's important to choose work that interests you, but the reality is that some fields just pay better than others. Ask yourself: What do you do better than most people you know? That is probably what you will enjoy and make money at. Studying those skills, going to school, getting training, and finding mentors are critical elements. Help from a career counselor or therapist can help you clarify your values, identify your aptitudes, and sharpen your vocational skills to maximize your lifetime earnings.

2) **Keep a budget** – To avoid the financial anxiety of being deeply in debt, you must know how much you earn and how much you spend, always spending less than you earn. Don't use credit cards except for an emergency – if you can't afford something, save up until you have enough money to buy it. Don't buy it on credit on the hopes that you will "someday" pay it off – many people never do. If you always earn more than you spend, you raise your self-esteem by developing emotional intelligence skills such as delayed gratification, impulse control, and working toward a rewarding goal.

3) **Save for your future** – Putting a percentage (ideally 10%) of your salary in your employer's 401-K retirement program can build savings quickly. Ask your Human Resources Department at work if you have one of these, and get investment advice from the plan's advisor if you do. You could also choose a specific amount each month to put into a bank savings account (perhaps via direct deposit of your paychecks). Saving for your future is critical for your retirement years that come sooner than we think. The interest this money will accrue over decades in your working

life will really add up, and the sooner you start, the dramatically better off you'll be. Even if you're only 18 or 20 years old, it's critical to try to save a standard 10% of your income. Financial management books as far back as the 1920's suggest that if you save just 10% of everything you make, you will likely have a comfortable retirement. You can relax knowing that your future is secure. The sooner you start, the better.

4) **Fix money leaks** – For one month, make a list of everything you spend. Look at the big expenditures. Are there wasteful "money leaks" that you need to fix? Reduce your monthly fixed costs by finding cheaper ways of getting things, like using coupons at the supermarket, finding stations with cheaper gas, or changing phone companies. Cut back on areas that take more than their fair share of your budget.

5) **Be "fiscally fit"** – If you have a bad credit score from missing or sending late payments to credit cards or utilities, learn how to fix it. There are books such as The Money Book for the Young, Fabulous and Broke by Suze Orman that can help. Keep your financial commitments by "paying yourself first" each month to your savings, and paying all of your bills on time and in full every month. Fulfilling your commitments and keeping your word are great ways to raise self-esteem. By taking responsibility, you build self-confidence, improve relationships with others, and feel good in the knowledge that you are respected and reliable.

6) **Build protections**—Getting in trouble with the IRS by not filing your taxes can lead to fines and even jail. Protect your assets by carrying insurance – such as car insurance (liability and collision, to protect your car and to protect you if you are sued), renter's or homeowner's insurance (in case of a fire or robbery), health insurance (in case of a sudden illness, or accident, or just routine care like a physical or weekly therapy!) and disability insurance in case you can't work your regular job. Make paying the appropriate insurance premiums a priority in your budget. A good insurance broker/advisor can advise you on this. Having insurance against the most common risks for your sex, age, and profession minimize your anxiety, provide reassurance, and restore hope if unfortunate events ever happen to you. Building protections during good economic times can help "buffer" you

from the challenges that come with the inevitable economic downturns, including recessions.

7) **Give back to the Universe** – Inspirational and motivational author Jack Canfield, in his classic book, <u>The Success Principles,</u> suggests that we "tithe" our income – which is to set aside a certain percentage of your choosing (such as 5-10%) for giving away to charities or causes you care about. This creates a wonderful good feeling of altruism, "karma," and can give a sense of pride and self-esteem by helping others who are less fortunate. People who do this often report amazing stories of great things happening to them, as if the Universe is taking note of your generosity and taking care of you in return.

While all of these are practical tips, don't forget to consider the psychological meaning of money. Louise Hay offers a wonderful audio recording lecture on CD on "Prosperity" (www.HayHouse.com). She implores us to explore our beliefs about money, and how they came into being – often from our parents, including a fundamental belief in abundance – or, unfortunately, "poverty-oriented thinking." Learning to believe, if you don't already, in "the abundance of the universe," is a wonderful way to develop peace of mind. It's similar to a basic trust versus a basic mistrust, or even seeing the glass as "half full" versus "half empty." It doesn't mean being foolhardy, but a basic trust that the universe is good and will provide for you can be encouraging and motivating in your commercial endeavors.

Like all financial advice, you should see a professional financial advisor before making any important decisions. There are many other ways to become financially successful, but these seven tips are among the most practical. Putting all these in practice can help you to have the life you want.

Prosperity

While a section on "Prosperity" might seem redundant to follow a discussion on "Money", they are actually very distinct topics, which is why each of these gets its own exploration.

As mentioned before, Louise Hay's audio CD on "Prosperity" (www.HayHouse.com) is the best treatment on this topic I know, though there are many good resources that address this. Hay describes how prosperity can certainly be about money, but it can also be about health, energy, beauty (of the self, or the world around you), companionship (either platonic or romantic), joy, time (having leisure, not being rushed and therefore "poor in time"), and of course the many variations of money, which can be our salary, new purchases, or belongings left over from long ago.

When I work with clients on prosperity, I assess all of these areas. Part of having the life you want is to identify where you are strong and where you are lacking in all of these areas, and learning to live in gratitude for the areas that are fine, and learning to cultivate and expand the areas that are less developed.

Prosperity in health is one of the greatest treasures a person can cherish. Achieving optimal health, while it incorporates very much of the spirit, I think is still somewhat mechanical. It has to do with the optimal functioning of our bodies as organic machines, with many moving parts. Health is defined sometimes as merely the "absence of pathology" meaning that nothing is broken, tweaked, weakened, damaged, swollen, infected, or dysfunctionally altered. Medicine, one could say, is intervening surgically, pharmacologically, or mechanically with things that are. Sometimes what stands between us and "health" is an intervention utilizing one or more medical techniques, under the guidance of a trained, appropriate medical professional – from an MD, to an RN, DO, or chiropractor, or even a Reiki practitioner, massage therapist, or shaman. Another aspect to health is just giving the body – your body – what it needs to thrive. I personally think I need a small amount of full-sugar Pepsi to function, just due to my own individual alchemy. Other people could identify something that they feel is their special key to health, which is part chemistry, part superstition, and part tradition.

If you don't feel healthy, vibrant, or energetic, it's time to do some troubleshooting. Ask yourself, What is the pathology? What is "broken" that needs to be fixed? If you can't answer that, find someone who can help identify the etiology of what ails you. Identifying a problem is the first step toward fixing it. Keeping patience enough to go at a steady pace without becoming impatient, yet being eager for change enough to keep you moving and motivated, is a delicate balance. Throughout, keep a vision of yourself as living in optimal health. If others can do it, you can, too. Oftentimes physical dis-ease is a sign that something is not well within our spirits, and if our spirits improve by embracing an Attitude of Gratitude, letting go of negative beliefs about the Self or others, giving more to others, we find that we feel better across the board. Allow yourself to feel "rich" in health, and discover through trial-and-error what kind of foods, exercise, thoughts, spirituality, socialization, and habits contribute to feeling good, when you feel good.

Prosperity can also be about beauty. Not just "being a pretty person" – while that is nice, it's hardly the key to life. Beauty can be about taking pride in your appearance, particularly when you adopt a personal style of hair, clothing, and accessories that expresses your wonderful unique individuality, but it's also about feeling prosperous in noticing and enjoying beauty around you. If we look at the world through the eyes of a Connoisseur of Beauty, we find much to see. Trees, flowers, architecture, fashions, physiques/figures, faces, art, pop culture, Nature – are a regular art gallery to appreciate, on our morning walk or our jaunt outside the office to grab lunch. It's all around us, and appreciating it is free. That kind of prosperity cuts across all classes and incomes, because it's available to all of us.

One can be very rich, or very poor, in companionship. If the number and quality of your friends were like a bank account, what would your balance be? If we "earn" prosperity in the moments we spend time with others, and we "lose" it if we are alone when we don't want to be (as opposed to valuable times of solitude when we DO want to be), then what is your balance? If you're overdrawn, it's time to make some deposits to your Companionship account. Very often I tell my clients who are looking for additional companionship to do things with, like go to the movies, those kinds of relationships start as a by-product of doing something you would normally do anyway. You might start out taking a local cooking class by yourself because you're interested in learning more about a certain kind of cooking. And that in itself is a valuable experience. But maybe you also take an interest in someone who is taking the class with you, and casual conversation working together in class leads to this person becoming a new "dinner buddy" that you see each week to try a different restaurant. Boom; instant deposit into the Companionship bank account! Sometimes becoming "richer" in friends is about knowing when to reach out and make a stranger into an acquaintance, and an acquaintance into a friend. Investing in them by taking a sincere interest in who they are, what they do, what is important in their lives, and why, can pay dividends back to you in the form of their friendship and companionship when you need it most.

Louise Hay's discussion of Prosperity included a statement that I love, when she said one can be very poor in Joy. Think about that. Think about the last week or so of your life, with work, domestic life, urban or suburban stress, and the whole routine. How much JOY was there in those days? My guess is not enough, as it is for way too many of us. Making and creating more joy in our lives is a commitment that we have to make to ourselves to do, for it sadly doesn't necessarily come naturally in our crowded, fast-paced world. Yet some people have mastered joy in their lives to an art form. I have several friends who have done this, and their daily status updates on Facebook attest to just how many joyful activities and experiences they create for themselves on a weekly, if not daily basis. Joy is another thing that is not restricted to any one socio-economic class, yet it certainly can help define our quality of life. Much of having a life prosperous in Joy is about making a point to have it be so. Making decisions about how to spend your free time and discretionary income plays a big role in this. Put joy first, the mundane second. That's a key to optimal living that I've seen a number of people master beautifully, and how "rich" they are for it.

Louise Hay also makes the point that we can be very poor in Time. When I first heard her say that, the statement hit me like a ton of bricks in how true it was. At the time, I was very poor indeed in Time, always rushing and feeling like I was running late from the previous task for whatever I was doing next. That's an impoverished way to live, with pressure and anxiety. Mastering time – even by learning and applying time management and productivity techniques— is one sure way to feel more prosperous about your life, and you haven't earned an extra dime. Believing in the abundance of the Universe, that there is time for everything and "it will all get done; it will all happen" as Hay says, is key. Much of this is simply over-estimating the time you think things will take. When you live in Los Angeles, as I do, it's almost impossible to over-estimate travel time. You just get less done because the traffic is so slow in most areas. But this is OK; you simply don't over-extend yourself, and you accept that the cost of time for many tasks is high. Don't try to do as much. If this feels impossible, it's time to simplify your life (Elaine St. James has an entire series of books on this topic that I recommend to my clients, with many practical tips on her entire "Simplify" philosophy, which are incredibly self-nurturing and affirming). An affirmation, inspired by the work of Elaine St. James and Louise L. Hay (among others) is, "I have all the time I need for all that I need and want to do." That is very empowering.

And then, of course, there is money. Being prosperous in just plain financial terms does have its advantages, and anyone who tells you differently is lying. It's just a fact, and as my clients in AA say, we must "live Life on Life's terms." Living life on life's terms means that we need money to function in our current capitalistic, commercial society, and part of having the life you want is having the money you want. Optimal life management means taking responsibility for our lives enough to create the salary or other income we want (such as "passive income" from some means, like investments). Prosperity in money is also about the belongings we purchase that we cherish. A good rule for spending is that if you don't CHERISH it in some way, don't buy it. Also, don't buy it if it doesn't "bring you up" spiritually and support your values, priorities, and goals for your life. Also don't buy it if you resent the price you're paying for it, or if you feel over-charged. Don't buy it if you feel it doesn't fit with your morals and values—some people will only buy products made in America to support the American economy and preserve American jobs, and others will not buy fur to prevent cruelty to animals, and still others won't patronize companies who pollute the environment or violate workers' rights. Conversely, patronizing an artisan, craftsman, skilled laborer, or designer whom you respect and admire can not only get you the goods and services you want, but can make you feel good about who you are patronizing with the Seal of Approval that is your discretionary dollar. Having an awareness of how you earn and spend money is part of feeling empowered and prosperous. It's also about valuing what we have, versus what we want.

Finally, one can feel prosperous in the things they own. You've probably seen the bumper sticker that says "the best things in life aren't things", and this is certainly true. Our experiences living in our world, our relationships with the people who mean much to us, the feelings that we savor throughout our lives are probably the most treasured things we "own." But it's also OK to feel grateful and joyful about "things" we like that make our homes comfortable and affirmative places to be in. I have a collection of antique toys, some from my childhood and some I acquired later, that are on prominent display in my home, and they never fail to generate curiosity, amusement, conversation, and even wonder. Just seeing them evokes positive memories of playfulness, fascination with how they were designed and made, the circumstances under which I acquired them, and a whole sampling of good feelings just in a glance at the shelf. This is something about my home that I cherish. I also have photos scattered throughout that are a symbolic reminder of important people and experiences, and these are cherished. I have souvenirs from travels around the world, and these give me a boost every time I see them, and remember an experience or feeling I associate with where and when I got them (gosh; it sounds like I have an awfully cluttered house, huh? It's just that I have created a home environment that is inspiring and nurturing for me). And this can be true for anyone, as our "things" are very subjective expressions of who we are. They are not "who" we are, but they represent us, and cherishing even our worldly possessions can be a part of feeling prosperous, in the context of all the others.

Do you have the life you want in terms of these items of Prosperity? If not, what would you have to do, believe, or allow to feel prosperous in these areas? What baby steps could you take to feel more prosperous in your "weakest link" area? Set some short-term goals for this, and work toward them. Use the affirmation, "I am prosperous in all the ways that are important to me."

Challenges: Finances

Being "not self-empowered" when it comes to finances is almost a cliché. I hear this from so many clients, and from friends, too. And there are so many ways that we dis-empower ourselves when it comes to money.

Many of my favorite authors have addressed this better than I. Louise Hay, Chellie Campbell, Casey Truffo, Lynn Grodzki, Suze Orman and others have implored their readers to really explore their historical beliefs about money, and especially about lack. Our beliefs about money will determine our relationship to it, for better or for worse.

Money certainly can be indicative of disparities in social power. One reason we all tend to want to "keep up with the Joneses" is our competitive nature as humans, but it's also a "drive" to maintain or increase social power. Ideas of the "haves" versus the "have-nots" have fueled social unrest and political controversy for millennia, and other books cover this topic in detail for those interested in history or economics. Perhaps the idea we should keep in mind here is just that these dynamics persist, and our lives will be affected by them. Part of being in society and making a meaningful contribution with our lives is doing our part to work for social justice to minimize the negative effects of the social imbalances of money that create an underprivileged class, most often through no fault of their own. This can be working for a charity, donating to causes we care about, or just paying our fair share of taxes without griping about it.

Perhaps the most important thing to remember about money, as challenging as it is to keep this in mind, is to remember that it is NOT a reflection of the value of our human worth. There have been rich scoundrels and poor noble folk, and noble rich and scoundrel poor. I know; I've worked with all of these in my career, and I am convinced that money and character of a person are truly independent variables!

We are disempowered about money when we give it too much attention, or too little. We are disempowered about money when we fear it, and it makes us a slave to it, rather than us understanding money as a means to an end, a currency, a resource to be exchanged.

We are disempowered about money when we are focused on lack, or carrying a negative belief that "money is the root of all evil", or that "rich people are evil", or even that the Poor are always noble. I've worked with some really poor people in various programs for the homeless who were greedy and underhanded. Not all rich people are exploitive and greedy, and not all poor people are noble and innocent. They are independent variables in the character of a person.

Self-empowerment when it comes to finances, much of the time, includes taking responsibility for our lives. How many times have I seen people (clients, friends, or family) be upset (disempowered) about money because they haven't bothered to read urban parking restriction signs, and then received expensive tickets for violating the clearly posted rules? How many clients have bemoaned a large past tax burden, when they haven't taken the responsibility to pay quarterly income tax installments as a self-employed person? How many clients have rung up large debt, indulging their every desire for goods, services, and travel, and then complain their credit card debt overwhelms them? How many people fail to discipline themselves to learn about long-term investment and the power of saving over a lifetime, then bemoan not having enough money for retirement?

Suze Orman's books and workshops address these issues very well. She tends to focus on how specifically women are not self-empowered, but other populations fall prey to this as well, as outlined in her book, The Money Book for the Young, Fabulous, and Broke. But I've worked with many high-income white male executives who are just as disempowered about money as these other populations are. Suze and others like her often get very emphatic about what to do, and what not to do, in order to achieve financial self-empowerment. I tend to do this, too. With the right thinking, organization, and especially self-discipline, finances are not that hard to manage. Without it, your life will feel disempowered and chaotic.

Go back and make sure you understand the seven ways to take care of your financial self. Think about which aspects of money management you are the LEAST comfortable with, and then seek out external resources to help you close those gaps. Use the resources (often in books) that will help you bridge the gap between what you know, and how you feel, about money, and how you would like to feel.

Being self-empowered about money can make us feel prosperous and relaxed, regardless of what our actual income may be. Bring humility to the process; don't be ashamed of what you don't know, but at the same time, don't let yourself be bitten in the butt by your own ignorance. There is no shame in admitting that you need help to understand budgeting, long-term planning, and how to choose among various investment resources. But there is a shame if your ignorance keeps you frustrated, longing, and broke.

Start with the affirmation, "I handle my finances skillfully and resourcefully", and then take action in concrete, behavioral terms. Start with the exercise, "If I were to become more financially self-empowered today, I would _____." And then do it. And do that over time, and you become solvent, relaxed, and prosperous, empowered to have the financial life you want.

Finances

Case Study: "Dale"

Dale was a client who had a long way to go in terms of being financially self-empowered. He had a wonderful home-based business as a website designer. Clever and technically savvy, he had built the most impressive websites for a long list of clients. His hourly rate was high, but he got it, because his portfolio of active online sites he designed was robust.

But Dale also had large credit card debt, owed tens of thousands in back taxes because he was "always so busy" making pretty websites that tax deadlines were the last thing on his mind, and who could find the overdue bills in the piles and piles of materials that grew in large towers on his desk? But at least he dressed well. If it weren't Prada, Hugo Boss, Louis Vuitton, Ferragamo, or Dolce & Gabbana, it didn't grace his body. Growing up poor and ashamed of his second-hand clothes he wore to school, as an adult he wouldn't wear a thing that wasn't the hottest fashion this season. He looked great – except for the tired eyes and drawn face that came from his financial worries. And the fights with his wife about why they couldn't afford to go to their nephew's wedding took their toll, too.

Working with Dale was a challenge. On the one hand, I felt so bad for this tired, weathered man in front of me. On the other hand, I saw Dale's stubbornness in failing to see how HE had created these circumstances for himself, and how only he could dig himself out.

We started with some cognitive work on his self-esteem, which was low, except in his ability to see himself as a talented professional. He had learned from being a teased kid at school to feel helpless and that life just sort of happened to him, rather than him steering his own course. As he learned to challenge the deeply held negative thoughts about himself, he began to be a little more proud of himself. He got increasingly sick of the mess that was his home office, and came in one day saying he had hired a professional organizer, who cleaned up the piles in one day. He also had put an ad out for a part-time assistant, who can help him pay bills on time while he was buried in his computer doing website designs. He identified a tax lawyer through a friend, and a years-long tax debt was whittled down to a manageable payment plan. He processed and came to terms with the trauma of being a poor, disheveled little boy, and learned that he had value, even if he were stark naked with nary a stitch of designer clothing.

We addressed the issue of his credit card spending by exploring feelings of deprivation from his poor childhood. We discussed concepts like delayed gratification and existentially valuing what he had, versus what he commercially yearned for. We differentiated between the inherent qualities he had as a person, versus the prestige of what he owned. I also taught him affect regulation (managing your feelings without becoming overwhelmed by them) and impulse control, especially when it came to purchases.

It took careful work in cognitive therapy to change his various negative thinking and attitudes, especially toward himself. It took a connection to many external resources that helped him with the practical problem-solving for cleaning up the financial mess and *keeping it that way*. But learn he did, and a wonderful addition to this work was decreased tension with his wife. And they did find a way to afford both a trip for their nephew's wedding, and a side-trip for a long-overdue second honeymoon.

I'm inspired to repeat about therapy what AA says about its program: "Keep coming back; it works if you work it."

Family

Having the life you want in terms of family is a daunting challenge. This is mostly because it's not "all about you;" there are others involved, and family dynamics are nothing if not a collective, interpersonal, dynamic process. You can't choose the family that you're born (or adopted) into. But you can learn to make the most of it. One of the ways our lives can be enriched is by experiencing the many different ways we can achieve a sense of "family." I've heard one informal definition of family from a friend who said a family is where two or more people gather in love and mutual commitment to well-being. That's pretty simple, but very powerful. It also validates the idea that there are all kinds of "families"—male-male, male-female, female-female—"love makes a family."

Our most obvious concept of family for most of us is our family of origin. Family of origin has to do with the circumstances of our birth, our natural genetics (what a lovely game of random-chance that is!), and for some of us, it includes as well our offspring (natural or adopted). This usually includes a relationship with parents or primary caretakers (which most mental health professionals agree is absolutely critical to our development, but can be mothers or fathers), siblings (who are valuable in that they are "like us" and "unlike us" at the same time), and extended family (where aunts and uncles are "like" parents, and yet so "unlike", too). The importance of grandparents has always been huge to me, as they give us a sense in a cultural and historical context of where we came from. All of my grandparents lived to be well past ninety, and I consider this one of the richest blessings of my life to this day. There isn't a day that goes by that I don't evoke in myself some wisdom, amusement, or perspective that they gave me. In many ways, they taught me how to live. For people who don't have living grandparents, I encourage them to have some sort of connection to living people from previous generations, for an enlightenment of how life was for them in past eras. They don't have to be blood relatives; they can be people who serve as "substitute grandparents."

Our sense of self – one of the cornerstones of self-empowerment – very much comes from our relationship to our family – particularly our parents. We learn from our family about who we are through a series of rituals, teachings, educational experiences, and interactions that occur in our homes. We learn about culture, values, and civilized living this way.

But while family of origin has deep emotional impact on all of us, in all kinds of good and bad ways from birth to adulthood, once we achieve adulthood, it becomes not only about Family of Origin, but, also Family of Choice.

Families of Choice are the interactive, mutually supportive bonds that we make with others who have something in common with us besides blood and genetics. In all cultures on Earth, we form communities and affiliations. There is more on this later in the chapter on Community, but families of choice come from our desire to form bonds with those who value something we value. A Family of Choice can be the collection of loving, supportive people we cultivate to be our Social Support System, especially if we live far away from blood relatives. These are the people who share our recreational time, our hobbies, our holidays, and the activities outside of work that we find meaningful. We can also have a Family of Choice at work, where we feel a sense of brotherhood with our colleagues – and maybe even some maternalism or paternalism about a female or male boss (these dynamics can be tricky and misleading, though – your boss is NOT your parent!).

But both Families of Origin and Families of Choice support our self-empowerment by giving us people to "bounce off of", because we don't grow and develop in a vacuum. People are by nature social animals, and nearly all animals have "families" they employ for support and even survival.

Having the life you want in terms of family means making the most of the people who ARE available to you (as opposed to ones who are missing, deceased, or otherwise unavailable) and resolving conflict with the ones who are a source of distress. In these situations, self-empowerment means accepting the other person, negotiating with them for a new (more functional) relationship, or sometimes distancing for your own survival and well-being. There is nothing wrong with setting firm limits on contact with a family member (origin or choice!) who is abusive.

It is also important to remember that you are a member of other people's families, and are expected to give support to them as well. The opportunity to give support can also be validating and empowering.

Taking responsibility to make the most of your family of origin, and to cultivate the family of choice that you need for your life circumstances (age, gender, culture, profession) is important to having the life you want. No one of us operates alone; we are all at the center of the spokes of a wheel, where we receive and give support to our many types of families that make the wheel go around.

Challenges: Family

In my practice, I see quite a number of examples of what can undermine self-empowerment when it comes to family. Anyone who can identify with the dynamics of a "dysfunctional" family can relate. I think the pitfalls are many, and they include:

Toxic Parents

The reason that family of origin conflicts can be so painful is because the relationships are important to us in the first place. The abandonment rage that a person can experience from an absent, neglectful, or even abusive parent is one of the purest forms of pain a person can experience. It takes enormous personal work (and often therapy) to heal emotional injuries of this kind. I always say that we are all as neurotic as our parents were deficient in parenting skills; wherever they made mistakes in parenting is much of where our "imperfections" come from.

It is unfortunate, but very possible, to have an adult relationship with parents who are truly toxic to your mental health and well-being. Adult children who were abused as children might have unrepentant parents who deny or even defend their abuse – either because they were the perpetrator or because they were the silent co-perpetrator who allowed the abuse to continue, abdicating their required role as a parent to protect their child.

Hypercritical parents who intrusively intervene or are constantly saying negative criticisms, often unsolicited, are undermining to an adult child's career or their choice of spouse/partner, home, appearance, etc. all can undermine self-empowerment.

Susan Forward, Ph.D. does masterful analysis of these phenomena in her book, Toxic Parents: Overcoming Their Hurtful Legacy and Reclaiming Your Life. I use this as one of the seminal "text books" of my practice, and I refer clients to it frequently. It addresses somewhat separate issues of physical, emotional, and sexual abuse, but the abuses have many elements in common. Dr. Forward is big on encouraging systematic confrontation, and I have seen clients follow her model with liberating success and "re"-self-empowerment.

I have worked with some extreme cases of clients with very toxic parents, and the image that I always describe is from "Superman" comics. In the Superman mythology, his only vulnerability on Earth is when he is exposed to Kryptonite, the rock fragment remnants of his home planet, Krypton, which exploded as he was being transported to Earth. This green, glowing, radioactive isotope is toxic to him, and if he is near it, he will weaken; with prolonged exposure, he would die. Toxic parents can be like this. If we are near them, we weaken and lose our sense of self. If we are constantly around their toxicity, we lose most of what makes us, "us", and lose our dreams, hopes, and goals of a satisfying life.

How does Superman mitigate this? Two things: Distance and Containment. If he is far away from the Kryptonite, he can't be harmed by it. If he contains the Kryptonite in lead, such as a lead box or lead safe, it can't harm him. Well, the same goes for toxic parents. If we have distance – limited visits, for short terms, perhaps staying in nearby hotels and not "under their roof" for proximity and their "home-turf advantage", then maybe their toxicity doesn't rub off too much. Or, there is containment: setting limits about how we insist to be treated. No negative comments about your spouse/partner allowed. No negative comments about hair style, makeup, jewelry, clothes, choice of accessories, where we live, what we do, what hobbies we have, or how we spend our own hard-earned money. Most of the time, the distance/containment strategy works to protect us from being emotionally undermined or re-injured from old abuse patterns. However, in some cases, such as toxic parents who are extremely narcissistic, unrelentingly critical, involved in criminal activity, or who deny or defend past abuse, it may become necessary to have what I call "total estrangement" or "emancipation." I've only seen this necessary in a handful of clients over 18 years of clinical practice, but I have seen it – where, honestly, the best choice for the mental health and well-being of the client is a total estrangement from the toxic parents. No visits, no phone calls, no letters, no emails – nada. One client changed her name and moved overseas, which for her was positively symbolic, ritualistic, liberating, and extremely emotionally healing to escape the legacy of unrelenting abuse from Narcissistic parents who never really "got" why she "disappeared on us all of a sudden" (as she heard from second-hand sources).

Of course, the clients who took extreme boundary measures did struggle a bit with guilt. I've found this to be true, even in cases where my client, as the adult child, suffered severe abuse. I think this is because we are conditioned as children, like the old Bible commandment, to "honor thy father and thy mother." My "healthily haughty" response to that is, "Yeah, well, only if they deserve it." Abusive parents simply don't deserve it. Not until they appropriately acknowledge and take responsibility for the abuse that they caused, or allowed to be caused, and make strident and sustained efforts to make amends. Clients have sometimes had to come to terms with their guilt, and understand that self-empowerment – and good old-fashioned self-esteem – sometimes demand that they put themselves first, and prevent themselves from being emotionally re-injured by emotionally irresponsible parents. Sometimes, that's just part of being a grown-up.

Toxic Siblings

Just as parents can be toxic to adult children, we can also have toxic siblings. While more rare, I do see this in my practice. The failure of self-empowerment when it comes to siblings is when we allow dysfunctional relationships with siblings in our childhood to continue to negatively affect us in the adult present. Toxic relationships with siblings can manifest in lots of ways – constant, unjustified jealousy; dependence; guilt; manipulation; and envy. If we work overtime so that our freeloading brother can avoid getting a basic job, and we give him money, that's not self-empowerment. If we hold a grudge against our little sister because "Mom always liked her best", when we've both been adults for 30 years, that's not self-empowerment. If you begrudge your brother making a large salary, when he graduated from business school when you didn't want to bother applying to it, that's not self-empowerment – that's entitlement (expecting reward without work) and envy. I've seen lives practically ruined by sibling rivalry, which has deep psychological roots about love, acceptance, and bonding with parents, but as a seasoned, licensed clinician, what esoteric eloquent phrase can I offer about this? GET OVER IT! When we react in adulthood to a sibling as if we were still children, that's not self-empowerment. Self-empowerment when it comes to siblings is understanding that they are our generational peers, and will probably be here long after our grandparents, aunts, uncles, and parents are gone. They are it, next to us. Most likely, they will be the closest family (next to our own spouses/partners, and perhaps children) to us when it is our time to go. It behooves us to make friends with our siblings as early as possible, and as permanently as possible. Set boundaries where you need to, and don't give anything to a sibling that you will resent giving them. It's better just not to give it, or give it and let it go.

Siblings can be a gift. I consider my sister to be one of the greatest gifts of my life. She is a FAR better writer than I. Me. (Whatever; I told you she was the better writer). That is a sibling relationship that is to be cherished. I wish you the same.

Toxic In-Laws

The TV show, "Everybody Loves Raymond" took the idea of toxic in-laws and made a hysterical comedy of it. But the buttinsky tactics of mother Marie to daughter-in-law Deborah, if in real life, could have been devastating to Deborah and Ray's marriage. If you have a meddling in-law, your spouse/partner needs to address this. The original "Dear Abby", syndicated columnist Abigail Van Buren, used to write of this frequently. If you are married or partnered, your obligation is first to your spouse/partner, and not to your parents (unless you are being abused by that spouse/partner, then butting in by a parent or in-law is perfectly OK, to possibly save your life). Grow a pair of…scissors, and cut the apron strings. This is part of being a grown-up, too.

Toxic Adult Children

This can be very rare, but we are not self-empowered if we allow adult, freeloading children to run us financially dry, or for drug-addicted adult children to steal from us and take advantage of our good will. If you happen to have a "bad seed" adult child who is plagued by crime, drugs, or just plain laziness, it's time for some tough love. Being self-empowered means that you shoo the youngin's out of the nest for their own good. You've earned a life of relative leisure once the kids are grown, and it's your job to make sure they are grown – with nice, tall, long legs that walk out the door and out on their own, making their money, living their own lives. Sure, occasional visits are nice, but if your adult children are a source of pain, fear, debt, heartache, or stress, it's time to get some boundaries and be self-empowered to free yourself of any burden. They will be fine, trust me.

Occasional financial help is necessary for today's young generation, who are fighting for jobs that are otherwise outsourced to India. A little help now might be very valuable in the long run. But if they're not taking responsibility for being grown-up, at least the majority of the time, then you're not finished parenting yet and you have just a bit more to teach them: *independence*. (And it's YOUR independence I mean, not theirs!)

Problems with the Law

You're also not self-empowered when it comes to family relationships if there are problems with the law. If your parents, children, siblings, or other close relatives are involved in criminal activity, self-empowerment means that you fight VERY hard to have nothing to do with it. You might not feel comfortable turning them in, but certainly, don't allow any of their behavior to implicate you in wrongdoing. Self-empowerment is enforcing the values and the boundaries you choose for yourself, not the least of which is conducting yourself with integrity and social responsibility. It's OK to take a VERY hard line on this. If you get any flak, repeat like a "broken record" (if any of you remember how a broken vinyl Long-Playing Record used to sound before CD's): "This is my decision, and that's final." Self-empowerment, at the very minimum, is keeping yourself out of jail.

Problems with Money and Boundaries

Maybe it's just my Anglo upbringing, but as a general rule, neither borrower nor lender be. Money and its lending create weird boundaries in families, and can create silent expectations of submission and entitlement. Take responsibility for your life such that you develop a skill set so that you can always work, at least at something, so that you live within your means and never have to borrow money from a relative. Self-empowerment in families means that you share the joys of a common ancestry, history, culture, and gene pool. You don't share currency except in some very limited, conscious, self-empowered ways with a clear discussion of what is expected from each party.

Sometimes, our fellow family members are not toxic or abusive, just dysfunctional. Our parents did the best they could with what they knew; there is no definitive textbook for child-rearing, at least not in our parents' generation. Child-rearing is really "folk knowledge," and for better or worse, it depends heavily on skills and ideas passed down from generation to generation. Extremely few parents set out to create psychological problems for their children (and I have worked with some children of these kinds of parents). But it is not self-empowered to blame parents for everything. In adulthood, we can understand how our parents might have indulged themselves at our expense in our childhood (via their anger, resources, attention, laziness, alcohol, drugs, etc.). By adulthood, we can use critical thinking skills to understand the kinds of behaviors and values we learned from our parents that we want to keep, and which we want to discard. Each generation is an opportunity for a fresh start.

Self-empowerment when it comes to family means that it's a value-added process. Ask yourself if you would spend time with these people if they weren't related to you. Hopefully, the answer is yes. If not, that relationship is not going to really serve you in the long run. Self-empowerment is realizing this somewhat sad, even cynical fact: Never spend time with relatives you don't respect, and who give you a minimum modicum of respect. Life is too short. If they don't understand, who cares? It's your life. As I often tell my clients, sometimes self-empowerment comes with a bit of a "Healthy Haughtiness." You are under no obligation to spend any time with people who are overtly rude, abusive, or toxic. The loss is theirs.

Self-empowerment in families is also recognizing the ones you love and spending quality time with them. If you're not spending the quality time you want with the family members you like the most, then you need to empower yourself to change that. Make that phone call. Send that email. Ring that Skype call. Book that flight. Have the *family* life you want!

Family

Case Study: "Simone"

My client Simone came to see me for therapy at her wit's end in frustration over her current cocaine addiction. It had developed when she graduated college in the mid-80s, when she, like so many young people then, got into cocaine way over their heads. Another problem, in addition to the addiction itself, was that Simone was the daughter of a prominent businessman, who was as successful entrepreneur. Aggressive in business but generous in philanthropy, Simone's father, Gordon, cast a long shadow for anyone to follow, let alone his own daughter.

Simone was smart and talented as a book illustrator. Gifted, would be the word. But nothing she did, however impressive, ever really shined in the way that Gordon wanted. Is it any wonder, then, that Simone took respite in wild nights of party time with a group of outgoing friends who always knew the latest hot-spot?

But by middle-age, the 80s had passed, and most of the close friends Simone knew from that time had long disappeared. Some moved away; some got sober, got married, and had babies off in the suburbs, and no group of friends ever really took their place. What was left was a frustrated Simone, still mired in a cocaine addiction, long after the party was over and the other guests had left.

It was obvious that part of Simone's therapy had to be in support of her recovery from cocaine, and abstinence from it with the support of going to AA meetings, which Simone liked a lot. She felt at home there and always learned something from her peers. She even met Dirk there, a handsome biker who had an edge she found exciting, but was sober, kind, and stable in his employment. And he treated Simone like a queen – or the "princess" she was used to being on Gordon's generous trust fund.

It became obvious in Simone's therapy, though, that while she became sober from cocaine, her heartache continued because of issues in her sense of family. Her mother had passed away when she was in college, and she was an only child, so her only family was Gordon, who was often busy with business or travel.

Over time in Simone's therapy, she became more self-empowered in her family by understanding that while her father was famous in his own world, Simone was talented herself. She stopped "living in her father's shadow", and established her own graphic design company, which quickly became popular and profitable due to Simone's learning from her father and her own unique spin on developing a business. She communicated with Gordon in increasingly frank ways, and negotiated Gordon's support for Simone to live her own life and make her own name for herself. Impressed by Simone's boldness in asserting her needs, Gordon was sensitive and responsive – supporting Simone where she needed and wanted it, and leaving her alone to build her own life.

In time, Simone and Dirk had their own family, and while Dirk wasn't Gordon's first choice for a son-in-law, he realized it was Simone's decision and that Dirk made Simone very happy – not to mention that the two striking parents made very pretty grandbabies.

Self-empowerment when it comes to family means developing and cultivating your True Best Self, putting your needs first, and setting appropriate boundaries where they need to be with members of your family —whether Family of Origin, or Family of Choice.

Community

Community is one of my favorite words (being a social worker), because it has so many potential positive connotations to it. Being a part of any community is a sign that we are not alone; that who we are is part of a larger group of people who share that same trait. Our sense of belonging and community is among Maslow's famous Hierarchy of Needs. It's a higher-order, more subtle need – it's not as urgent as food, for example – but Maslow's point was that we need a sense of belonging to achieve optimal mental health, and, I would say, a sense of community (many of them, actually) to achieve self-empowerment. Developing a sense of community as a tool in self-empowerment means making conscious decisions as to which communities we want to affiliate and identify with in order to support our sense of self for this lifetime.

There are many types of communities that we find ourselves affiliated with, and these might change over time according to our emotional needs and priorities at different developmental stages of our lifespan.

Certainly, when we are first growing up, we emerge from our families into a geographic community. We are a part of a spot on the globe, influenced by the local temperature, moisture, culture, food, water, natural resources, and type of government. Most of our geographic communities can be broadly described, such as "urban" or "rural." Some are quite specific, such as those who grow up in say the Upper East Side of Manhattan.

Each of us belongs to a wide variety of "communities," just by virtue of being human and living our lives. It is important to developing a sense of self to understand the communities to which we belong so that we can focus on those that are important to us. These could be:

- The geographic community we call home
- Our spiritual or religious community
- Our race and ethnic background
- Our sexual orientation
- Our gender identity (male, female, or transgender)
- Our health status (such as Cancer Survivors, People Living with HIV/AIDS, Diabetics, or physically challenged)
- Our professions
- Our hobbies (Tennis Enthusiast, Guitar Player, Gourmet Cook, Amateur Magician, Rollerblader, Motorcyclist)

We have communities according to profession, such as being a physician, nurse, psychotherapist (my personal favorite), others in the healing community, or lawyer, paralegal, judge, or others in the legal community. We can be salespeople, accountants, editors, computer programmers, financial analysts, teachers, plumbers, carpenters, academics, or retail sales associates.

Beyond our sense of self and identity that comes from our family, our acceptance and standing in various communities reflect and help define who we are.

Sometimes, self-empowerment and having the life you want is consciously altering which communities to affiliate more strongly with, and which ones to distance from. This takes active intervention on our own behalf, by examining both changeable and unchangeable traits we have, and the values, priorities, interests, talents and aptitudes we have, to create an entire network of inter-affiliative bonds with others who share these traits to form a sense of collective identity and social support – a community.

Challenges: Community

One challenge in our sense of community can be when we are a part of a community, not by our own choice, that is not to our liking. A young, ambitious son or daughter might resent their small farm community and yearn for the opportunity to pursue a dream in a big city. A person raised in many different military bases might long for a steady home community in one place. A woman who becomes sober might realize she has to distance herself from a community of family and friends who over-indulge in alcohol. Part of self-empowerment is choosing the communities where we want to be – and where we don't.

Another lack of self-empowerment when it comes to community is, I believe, not having a sense of belonging to one. If you feel isolated from much of your life, it's because something has not empowered you to join with the many definitions of community that are around you. It's time to reach and out join the human race.

Everyone loves their "Me Time" alone, but if you're single, and even if you're married/partnered, but still isolated from the communities around you, you are living a somewhat impoverished life and you are dis-empowered from the community ties that could add to your quality of life.

To empower yourself in terms of community, think about what communities you are a part of, from the discussion in the previous section. Then, set yourself some small, manageable goals about becoming more involved in a group that might mean something important to you. Even if you're an introvert, there is still opportunity to be a part of various communities in your own special way, such as the internet.

Experiment with this idea: If I were twenty times BOLDER in my involvement in my various communities, what would I do? How would that change my plans for tonight? Tomorrow? This weekend? Later this year? Try to come up with one NEW scheduled activity to involve yourself in a sense of community.

I bet you have fun with it. And I bet you feel self-empowered with a sense of belonging to one group, or more. Try it, and if I'm wrong, you can raspberry this page and say, "Ken, you're full of baloney, but I tried it anyway." And if I'm right, you're going to be spending less time reading books like this and more time enjoying some new friends in your community. I'm rooting for you.

Community

Case Study: "Gary"

One of my more recent clients, "Gary", was a man in his mid-40's whose story moved me very much. He had, by his own account, the "love of his life" in Ricardo, who was a bit younger at thirty-five. They were together for four years, and had been living together for a year, when Ricardo had a sudden heart attack one evening, completely unexpected, and died in his arms. It was revealed later that Ricardo had a congenital heart defect, that was completely undetected, but it was common that it struck men in their mid-30s.

Gary came to therapy for his acute grief, and his reported struggle that life had no meaning without Ricardo. He didn't see how he could go on after losing the love of his life. There are various techniques in therapy to help someone in acute grief, and much has been written about widows and widowers and how they adjust and move on with their lives after their loss. I used those techniques, and over time, Gary moved through each of very predictable, but still non-linear, stages of grief and mourning that widows and widowers tend to follow.

What was missing, though, was Gary's involvement in any sense of Community. Psychologically and emotionally, he came to terms with his grief and his status as a widower. His emotional health improved, but the last remaining challenge was that he was isolated and his lifestyle consisted of his job, and seeing only his best friend, Ivy.

At some point, Ivy became weary of being Gary's only social outlet, confidante, sounding board, and friend. Ivy confronted Gary, and stated she needed some respite for a while. Gary was upset about this, and told me so, and as much as I validated Gary's frustration, I had to say that I could see Ivy's point as well.

With gentle encouragement, I urged Gary to identify something in the community he could experiment with, to enlarge the confines of his life. Gary had always loved art, and had ample free time now that his business practically ran itself, so he visited various local museums, and looked into their volunteer docent programs. Gary loved the training, and he became an outgoing, knowledgeable, and popular docent who gave lively tours.

One woman he met on a tour, Amy, was part of a quilting club, and invited Gary. Gary made jokes about being a little old lady and doing quilting like it was the 19th Century, but he said with a twinkle in his eye and his characteristic cocked head, "You know, I actually ENJOY being a little old lady in a quilting club. And the stories they tell are actually pretty bawdy!" Gary smiled in a way that I hadn't seen before; it was like a light that went off in his eyes when Ricardo passed was being re-illuminated.

Gary was very spiritual, and told stories about how Ricardo seemed to be "with him" at times. Toward the end of his therapy, Gary said he felt connected to the world again. His work, Ivy, the museum, Amy, the quilting club, and now his yoga practice was making him feel whole again. That, and a meeting a man, Spencer, who opened his heart in a way that he thought he would never experience again.

"I'll always love Ricardo," he said, this time with a glint of "happy tears" in his eyes. "But last night I had this dream, where I was on a date with Spencer at my favorite restaurant, Le Fleur, which as I've said to you a million times is my favorite place on the planet. And Ricardo walked by, from across the room, and saw me with Spencer, and just gave me the biggest wink and smile. Then I knew, this guy is a keeper!"And the smile came back to his face, and the same glint in his eye.

For Gary, becoming self-empowered to reconnect with his community gave him the strength to re-connect with his Self, and to heal again.

Spirituality

The topic of spirituality in psychotherapy and coaching is a tricky one. I believe that self-empowerment when it comes to spirituality is having the presence to embrace – or reject – spiritual tenets as you see fit. Spirituality is meant to enhance our lives – not burden it, complicate it, or instill a lot of guilt. Burdens, complications, and guilt are not conducive to self-empowerment.

I start from the idea that all spiritual traditions have value, including the ones I am vehemently against, such as those that advocate physical, emotional, psychological, legal, cultural, or political violence. These abound in our world – religions that suppress women, denigrate gay, lesbian, bisexual, or transgender people, those that coerce people into political submission, those that exploit the money or well-being of others for their organizational gain (usually benefiting the top leaders), and ones that use mind-control tactics and soul murder, such as cults.

That said, spirituality can be a wonderful asset to a person's life and can give it a sense of purpose and a profound meaning. It can be the very cornerstone of self-empowerment, by giving a reason for living every day, according to deeply held spiritual principles – even if the spiritual values are more secular and involve a commitment to a secular humanism.

Spirituality is involved in the rites of passage of adulthood. Part of growing up is using our adult emotional intelligence skills of critical thinking to examine the spirituality or religion in which we grew up, usually under the authority of our parents in our household of origin. We must evaluate our "original spirituality" and decide which parts of it we want to keep, which parts we want to modify, and which parts we want to discard altogether. We transition from the spirituality of our parents' home, to the community of spirituality that we want to embrace in the world around us. Even Secular Humanism, an increasingly popular movement, is a type of spirituality in that it de-emphasizes concepts such as the soul or an afterlife, in favor of the spirit of the Brotherhood of Man (which includes women) while we are alive.

Spirituality's role in self-empowerment is profound. Just the ability to consciously choose a spiritual orientation that is in keeping with our evolved beliefs is an act of self-empowerment. We choose what beliefs, rituals, practices, priorities, and values that we want to adhere to, and these usually add up to involvement in some form of organized spiritual community where we share beliefs with like minds, but not always. As contradictory as this may sound, sometimes a spiritual affiliation can just be a group of individuals who think as individuals, who are united only by their dis-affiliation with any one spiritual group, tradition, or religion.

Spirituality in self-empowerment means believing in something "higher" than one's self, and asserting a certain loyalty to it. For some, this can be "God" or merely a "god"; it can be "the" Goddess, or "a" goddess. It can be the Higher Power, mentioned in many Twelve Step programs. It can be "the universe." It can be "Fate." It can be "the heavens" or the collective "gods." The conceptualizations of a purpose higher than ourselves are countless, across history, geography, and cultures.

Spirituality can certainly empower us by giving a sense of purpose to our lives, both professionally and personally. I have been influenced by many very "benevolent souls" who applied their spirituality to both personal and professional endeavors. My sister, a leading animal rights activist and author (Jill Howard Church), demonstrates this so inspirationally and beautifully. Her values include working to preserve the dignity and protection of animals from fear, pain, exploitation, and unnecessary or wasteful death. This guides her personal life in how she sees the world around her, but it also influences her decision to dedicate her professional life to these values.

Another example is my grandmother, who was a teacher of first grade for thirty years. She was a devout Southern Baptist, but her commitment to live in the example of Christ and give from the heart to others included imparting knowledge and supporting the development of the very youngest of our society's members at a time in life when they certainly needed it. Her dedication to this cause was profound, and it was, in part, informed by her spirituality by living in service to others. I believe that if a person cannot explain their life's work, even their job, at least in some part in spiritual terms, they might not have the professional self-awareness that would be ideal. We should all be bringing at least a little bit of service, love, and a "higher" sense of our purpose to our daily work.

Spirituality's power as a sense of comfort that empowers us to cope with adversity also can be profound. At times of stress or even tragedy, adaptive coping psychologically can easily involve the role of spirituality in how we understand, interpret, and survive the events. If we believe that what happens to us in life has a meaning beyond the immediate circumstances, perhaps even beyond our earthly comprehension, it can help us cope in the short term and heal in the long term. Classic books such as Viktor Frankl's <u>Man's Search for Meaning</u>, among others, explore this idea.

Spirituality is also a form of guidance. A building development might have an overall project plan. A non-profit organization might develop a Mission Statement that guides its existence, shepherded by its Board of Directors, executives, and staff. A company might develop a set of corporate principles, based on sound business practices. For people, we could benefit from following a template – from very general to very specific – that guides our behaviors and our approach to the world. An Orthodox Jew, for example, might adhere to certain dietary restrictions and wear certain clothes in keeping with that faith. A vegan's template might guide what they wear, eat, and use according to the welfare of animals. A Conscientious Objector might declare his or her faith when it comes to their involvement in war.

Spirituality can sometimes be a set of guiding principles that arbitrate our behavior. Even the popular phrase on the bumper sticker, "What would Jesus do?" is an example of how a faith might admonish its adherents to apply an objective guide for behavior toward their own behavioral choices – challenging them, for example, in the name of Christ to be charitable, forgiving, peaceful, and non-judgmental (ideally; not all Christians are non-judgmental). Mainstream Islam would encourage restraint and peace; radical Islam would encourage committing the most heinous acts imaginable in service to jihad, to punish perceived "infidels." Spirituality's function to serve as a guidance can be used, then, for dramatically positive – or dramatically destructive – purposes. Choose wisely.

Spirituality's ability to guide also applies to cultural considerations. Ways of eating, worshiping, dress, conducting business, raising children, and running a community all can be influenced by spirituality, or certainly by an organized religion. The ritual aspect of the expression of spirituality can be tremendously meaningful and comforting. The Eucharist, the ritual of ingesting bread and wine to symbolize the body and blood of Christ, despite (or perhaps because of) its vaguely cannibalistic overtones, is really a profound Christian tradition that embodies becoming one with the tenets of Christ, a communion of soul to deity. This can symbolize commitment to the faith on an individual basis, as well as sharing the ritual in a group service that presents an opportunity for people of the same faith to share a sense of community. Similarly, drawing a circle and performing outdoor chants or dances by firelight to symbolize different times in the Wheel of the Year might be practiced by Pagans or Wiccans, to honor and celebrate the natural cycles of the Earth. Rituals are the cultural observances that give meaning, tradition, celebration, and significance to the events of our lives in a way that elevates our lives from the mundane and gives us all a chance to celebrate being alive in the world around us. While this can be strictly cultural (such as Valentine's Day, of no real spiritual significance except vaguely related to a Catholic saint), or national, such as St. Patrick's Day, it can also include the rituals of Christmas and Easter (both Christian) or Samhain or Yule (both Pagan) as religious examples.

Beyond ritual, spirituality can also be a philosophy to guide our work, relationships, and hobbies. I think the connection between spirituality and work is especially profound. Many spiritual traditions and religions emphasize "being of service", which is found in the teachings of Christ, Confucius, Buddha, Gandhi, Martin Luther King, and others. Alcoholics Anonymous, in its largely Judeo-Christian spiritual emphasis, strongly emphasizes being of service as a way of liberating the self-centeredness of the tyranny of addictions. All of the helping professions (doctors, dentists, social workers, nurses, counselors, clergy, public policy advocates, volunteers) have a strong sense of being of service, then applied to a particular problem or niche of society. Having and practicing at least some form of spirituality, and being able to articulate how one's spirituality influences daily life, is a form of self-empowerment that gives meaning to both work and play.

Finally, spirituality gives a perspective that there is something beyond this life. For some traditions, it is a true Afterlife. A Hindu might revere the concept of reincarnation. For others, it is a consideration of a plane of existence beyond the usual rat-race. Understanding that our planet is only one of millions in the Universe, that everyone alive today follows generations of those who have come before us, and that people will go on long after all of us currently here are gone, certainly gives us perspective (albeit a sobering one). It can certainly make one "not sweat the small stuff", as the popular self-help book series by Richard Carlson, would encourage us to do!

To be maximally self-empowered via spirituality, I would survey the landscape of the many belief systems, faiths, traditions, and cultures available to the current world, and even in history. Find which ones align with your inner voice that ring true for you, and practice them. You can visit a church, synagogue, meeting hall, meditation center, ritual meeting, cultural center, historical site, or natural setting. You can read a book, listen to a CD, watch a video, hear a lecture, attend a service, download a podcast, read a brochure, or talk to others. Self-empowerment means that we are free to choose our spiritual orientation, without coercion, criticism, pressure, or undue interference from others. And if a spiritual tradition encourages you to think or do something that is outside of your value system, reject it. This is part of your responsibility as an adult, to not be conned by influence, nor pressured to serve an organization so that its members might be made rich, powerful, influential, or martyred. Spirituality should be a value-enhancing addition to your life; if a spiritual practice doesn't raise your quality of life in some way, forget it. It is perfectly OK to be a secular humanist and refuse to participate in any organized, or even un-organized, spiritually-based group. Being self-empowered means that these are your choices.

Challenges: Spirituality

A lack of self-empowerment when it comes to spirituality is evident everywhere. People in Alcoholics Anonymous would say that anyone currently suffering in the throes of an addiction – to alcohol, crystal meth, cocaine, heroin, gambling, sex, shopping, eating, etc. – is having a "crisis of spirituality", and their program teaches them how to re-connect with their profound spiritual sense of self in order to achieve recovery from the addiction.

People who live their lives in a rather banal existence of working in a job they don't really like, living in a place they don't really call home, and being around people they don't really love and who don't really love them, could be said to be having a crisis of spirituality in their ability to live their lives in the context of a higher purpose.

People who are enslaved by the various cult-like religions, who are giving too much of their time, certainly their money, and even the freedom of their mind, could be said to be particularly dis-empowered in their spirituality.

People who are capitulating to the demands of their chosen religion, even though the religion's values ask them to do something that isn't in congruence with their values, can be said to be dis-empowered spiritually. This can include women who are suppressed by a religion that is inherently male-dominated or sexist, or people who are told to hate gay and lesbian people in their name of their religion when this might mean being asked to hate their own children, brothers, uncles, aunts, neighbors, or best friends.

Anytime that our spiritual practice is not in line with who we are, what we believe, and how our values are determined, we are spiritually dis-empowered. Reclaiming our spirituality, then, is clearing our minds of how we were raised, what we were told in the very specific time, place, and culture of our developing years, and starting with a clean slate. What do we believe happens when we die? What are the most important guiding principles to follow that inspire us for our whole lives? What should the relationship be among people, animals, and the environment? What do my spiritual beliefs tell me about what to do, or not to do, when it comes to other people, and how to relate to them?

These kinds of guiding questions can help us refine what our adult chosen spirituality affiliation is – including, perhaps, not much at all. It is also self-empowered to choose to adhere strongly to the tenets of any particular spiritual or religious tradition. That is the beauty of living in the United States, at least, in that the nation was founded with a strong separation between its government and its many spiritual traditions, churches and religions. Despite various controversies, the USA remains a place where, to paraphrase Thomas Jefferson, our neighbors can worship one god, or twenty, and it neither lightens my purse nor eases my toil. In other words, Jefferson implied that we function as a pluralistic society, where each person is free to choose whatever spirituality they want, including none, and the government will not involve itself in these choices. I find that thinking, philosophy, and national policy incredibly progressive for Jefferson's time, the 18th Century. In this way, we are a nation of self-empowered people when it comes to spirituality.

Part of living the Self-Empowered Life is the ability to apply critical thinking to lots of situations, and coming up with how we feel about what is right for us. Take a moment to evaluate how you feel about your spirituality. Are your thinking, practice, and approach to your spiritual orientation meeting the profound needs of your mind and heart? If not, start to brainstorm the changes you could make to achieve that. Could you do more of something? Do you need to do less of something? Do you need to contact someone to cultivate a relationship? Do you need to distance yourself from a person or people who do not meet your needs?

These kinds of self-reflective questions, and the courage to make adjustments so that you are living your best life, can help you to Have the Life You Want, in spiritually congruent and profound ways that energize and fuel your life, and give it meaning beyond the daily routine.

Spirituality

Case Study: "Jenny"

My client, "Jenny", represents an important lesson in self-empowerment when it comes to spirituality. Jenny was about thirty, a creative, avant-garde type, who really "danced to her own drummer" in her manner of hair, makeup, and dress. But her history explained a lot of this: she was raised in a "fringe" cult with her parents, growing up in the 1970s in a commune as the child of a counter-culture mother and father. Jenny felt forced growing up to believe the cult's dogma. The cult had a lot of money and power, and any kind of dissonance to cult life was not tolerated. As Jenny grew up, she began to question the cult's activities, and eventually went away to college and felt a sense of escape. Her parents were enraged that she didn't continue in the cult as an adult, and Jenny became estranged from her family and lived on her own, in another city, with no contact with her family of origin.

As an adult, Jenny wanted nothing to do with any religion or any spirituality. The cult's harsh tactics made Jenny wary of anything that smacked of organized religion. As other stressors mounted as an adult, Jenny fell into drug addiction. Drugs were an easy route to peace for Jenny, escaping unwanted negative emotions. Over time, she developed a serious addiction to alcohol and cocaine.

After hitting her personal rock-bottom, she joined Alcoholics Anonymous (AA). At first, the talk of "God" and some of the rituals were profoundly triggering for Jenny as reminders of the aggressive cult in which she was raised. But over time, she learned that the greedy cult and AA were very different. She received supportive fellowship from her peers in AA. She listened to the program's encouragement to believe in a "Higher Power" of her own understanding, not one foisted upon her by cult leaders.

Reclaiming her right to live with a spirituality that was right for her, Jenny balanced her secular values of being a good, generous person, with a unique set of spiritual beliefs and practices that suited her perfectly. For Jenny, self-empowerment in spirituality came in the balance of escaping a negative spiritual experience as a child, with a positive one as an adult, on her own terms.

Resources

When we discuss self-empowerment, we are simultaneously talking about resources. In my psychotherapy practice model, part of the structure for problem-solving to help a client improve his or her quality of life is understanding what resources are needed to reduce, mitigate, modify, or eliminate a stressful problem. Resources are the things – tangible or intangible, real or conceptual, internal or external, that we identify, cultivate, rally, energize, and *apply* toward the solution or alteration of a problem.

Examples of external resources might be books (like this one!), CDs, tools, computer hardware, computer software (files or disks), people, raw elements (earth, air, fire, water), personal people (parents, children, coworkers, neighbors, ancestors, friends, family) and professional people (doctors, therapists, nurses, teachers, consultants).

Examples of internal resources would be courage, curiosity, stamina, determination, wonder, joy, perseverance, intelligence, street-smarts, instincts, hunches, visions, discipline, focus, hope, patience, discretion, judgment, appreciation, gratitude, creativity, resilience, optimism, frugality, efficiency, generosity, kindness, and love.

It is a law of physics that for every action, there is an equal and opposite re-action. I believe this is true of life's challenges: Self-empowerment is the ability to identify, rally, and apply our internal and external resources toward the solution of our problems.

I believe that to judiciously identify, rally, apply, and enjoy the benefits of resources, especially external ones, we need a few tools:

Research

We need to be able to search the landscape of the world around us with a bloodhound's nose of curiosity to see if the right external resource for us exists. If we are learning how to edit our blog on WordPress.com, is there a book that tells us how to use the WordPress features? Maybe. We might need to do an online search for that on Google.com, or see if there are similar titles at an online book clearinghouse like Amazon.com or LuLu.com.

Selectivity

Sometimes there are various resources that might meet our needs, but we have to apply selectivity criteria to guide which one we choose. Do you want a male gynecologist whose office is two blocks from your office? Or a female gynecologist who is across town? Which one has been recommended by your friends? Which one has the better parking? Which one has the more efficient front-office staff for answering phone calls, making appointments, and getting the results of tests? All of these might involve selectivity skills to distinguish among resources.

Acquisition

In order for a resource to be effective and useful, it must be able to be acquired. If the book you want on Amazon is out of print, you could try a library or locate a rare book dealer, but if it's still not available, you can't use it. If the only copy left is water-damaged, you might not be able to read it. If the gynecologist across town is too expensive, you might not be able to see her. Part of what makes a resource useful is not only its existence, but also its accessibility with a reasonable outlay of our own resources of time and money. If this book were $1,000 per copy, many fewer people might get the benefit of it.

Application

You have to be able and willing to use the resource. If you identify the best home treadmill, and you can afford to buy it, and then it sits in your den and goes unused, the resource of a home treadmill is useless. If the book that you bought is full of jargon you don't understand, it won't help you. Get advice from friends, read about the resource online, read online reviews, read the instruction manual, or experiment. But make the resource useful in your own way, for you.

Evaluation

Evaluating the resource means measuring its effectiveness for achieving what its goal was to achieve. If you run on your treadmill to fix your hypertension and your blood pressure doesn't fall, you might need to try a different form of exercise and consider a different resource, like a blood-pressure-lowering medication (under your doctor's care, of course).

Storage

Resources can either be stored for future use, or discarded. Some people love to indulge in a Feng Shui tradition of reading a book, then giving it away to someone else (or selling it) if they feel they have read and understood the material, and don't need to store it on the shelf indefinitely, unless they want to refer to it again periodically later.

Self-empowerment in resources means the above-mentioned skills, and feeling empowered to seek out and apply new resources whenever needed to help face life's challenges. When addressing a problem, get creative with your brainstorming what external and internal resources you need to apply. These can include:

■   Health Issues: doctors, pharmacists, medications, nurses, social workers, websites, brochures, books, blogs, CDs, seminars

■   Life Transitions and Challenges: support groups, books, CDs, blogs, civic organizations, family history lore, library programs

■   Community Issues: neighborhood watch groups, community policing, the public library, civic groups, and cultural organizations

■   Business Issues: books, websites, consultants, networking groups, colleagues, professional/trade associations, biznik.com.

■   Personal Issues: Close siblings, former or current roommates, trusted neighbors, old and new friends, and of course, therapists and coaches!

Perhaps my favorite resource when it comes to feeling self-empowered to address life's challenges is PEOPLE. People can help us in a way that no other resource can. It's one of the reasons I work as therapist/coach, and one of the reasons why this resource requires the most cost investment, because it is the most profound. I don't know where I would be in my understanding and appreciation of life if it weren't for the people in my life, past, present and future, who helped me to be who and what I am today. There are some negative examples, but I prefer to focus on the positive examples of people who made a difference in my life, and it is their standard of example that I strive to emulate in order to help others as I was once helped.

Who are the prominent people in your life who made you what and who you are today? These can be family, friends, colleagues, professionals, teachers, neighbors, and others.

I'd like to give some examples of how valuable people can be as resources for self-empowerment by sharing with you some of the people who have been especially valuable to me. These include authors, such as the following:

Louise Hay – is the author of the classic self-help book, <u>You Can Heal Your Life</u>, and I became exposed to her work just after I graduated from college and was really working on developing my sense of self as an adult. She also led a "live" support group on HIV issues where I lived, which I attended several years before learning of my own diagnosis with HIV, just because I wanted to hear her speak on "loving the self." She was a lovely lady and an inspiring speaker, and to this day, she is still one of the authors I quote and recommend in my sessions with clients.

Jack Canfield – His book, <u>The Success Principles</u>, is the one I refer to as the "text book" of my practice, and is currently the book I refer to most frequently. The first chapter of that book, on taking 100 percent responsibility for your life, is a good part of the theme of this book, self-empowerment. His additional sixty-three principles for successful living draw masterfully on the inspiration of authors, speakers, and teachers who have come before him, and the overall catalog of helpful material it recommends makes it an encyclopedic resource. His seminars and coaching services are at the highest-end, accessible usually only to high-income people and corporations, but they are known to be of the highest quality. I don't know him personally (yet), but I imagine him to be a wonderful guy to know.

Susan Forward, Ph.D – Her book, <u>Toxic Parents</u>, is a classic for people who are recovering from various forms of parental abuse. Just her basic term, "abuse survivors", is something that I use many times in session. If a book can be a pathway to improved quality of life, this one is it. I also use this as an adjunct to individual therapy.

Susan Jeffers, Ph.D. –Wrote the book, literally, on fear. <u>Feel the Fear and Do It Anyway</u> is extremely valuable in addressing one of the most common of human vulnerabilities – fear – which is really the opposite of self-empowerment. Accessible and very practically useful, it also a "required reading" for many of my clients.

Lynn Grodzki, LCSW, CPC – Lynn writes books and other media resources that guide and develop therapists and coaches. Without her support via these materials, I would never have developed all the joy in my work that I experience every day, for she taught me how.

Casey Truffo, MS, MFT – Perhaps my highest praise goes to this lady – and I do mean lady. Classy, knowledgeable, funny, and vastly inspirational, her role as the founder of the International Therapist Leadership Institute, along with extremely valuable materials to coach the careers of therapists, coaches, and other healers – teaching us all to "make a living, while making a difference" – makes her a true Thought Leader in the field. In self-empowerment, it is important to identify and put your trust in teachers who are worthy of our faith, to buy their materials, follow their instructions, and reap the benefits of doing so. Casey's materials have been that resource for me, and every time I spent a cent in my life that is from my livelihood as a therapist and coach, there is a part of her in that cent, because she taught me how to earn it! In every business, in every career, we have "angels" who help us grow, without which we wouldn't fully develop our Professional Self. For me, Casey has been that person.

As much as I appreciate these professional inspirational people and their related resources, a discussion of "people as resources" to educate, inspire, develop, support, and sustain us would not be complete without reflecting on what our family members mean to us. No family is perfect. Some are great, some are neurotically dysfunctional, and some create horribly abusive environments. Some families are fraught with odd jealousies, long-held resentments, conflicts, and quirks. Some families are drunk on alcohol. Some indulge in racism or are obnoxious to their neighbors, while others contribute vital advancements to many fields, or are pillars of the community.

Most families, including mine, were a mixture of some of these, but as a self-empowered adult, I choose to focus on the more positive aspects of my family experience. I choose to see the positive qualities in others, and I encourage you to do the same. As the Alcoholics Anonymous saying goes, "take what you want, and leave the rest." You can do that with your family. Knowing what has inspired or educated you from your family can contribute to your self-empowerment as an adult.

I want to leave this chapter, and indeed this book, with one last story of a human resource, because it's a story about leaving inspiration to the ones you love, when it comes time to part.

One of the most significant experiences in my life was my time spent as an avid, even obsessive drama student at my high school outside of Washington, DC. It was the high school that I was geographically assigned to, but I believe was spiritually assigned to, as well, for it was known for its exceptional drama department, one that kids from other school districts wanted to commute into (one very close friend from a wealthy and influential family did just that). It was exceptional because of its director, a drama teacher and the director of the school's many renowned productions of sometimes controversial plays, which she dared to produce in a high school for the educational and artistic challenge of it. She was Joan C. Bedinger, a West Virginia native with a lyrical, charming Southern accent, a dramatic visage that was part witch and part goddess, with flowing hands that danced in the air in emotionally punctuated gestures that Mesmerized as they delightfully illustrated an endless string of educational, observational, and inspirational pearls of wisdom. Such was the case for the four years of my constant rapture of her endless teachings.

She would inspire us with tireless artistic direction, but the final stages of the final rehearsals of any given production would wind down, the last run-throughs run, and the time for bestowing our new production on the public would arrive. Her last admonishment, for every production, every show, was this: *Make Every Moment Count.*

Toward the end of my senior year, as the last Spring projects were performed in the advanced Level 4 drama class, in a hot, then-un-air-conditioned public school auditorium, she lowered her voice, and began her speech: "You all are going in lots of different directions soon. Your various colleges and paths are spread all over the country." (Especially mine; I was soon off to leave the East Coast permanently, in my transplantation to a new life in Los Angeles, where I have been ever since.) "And much of what you've learned here will be forgotten. It must be. It's too much; it's too long, and too much happens. But if you remember nothing else of what I've taught you here, during this time here, remember this..." And, in that moment hanging in the muggy summer air, I knew that whatever she said next, I would remember for the rest of my life. And she said, *"Never Stop Growing."*

And I haven't. And I beg you not to, either.

Since she left all of us with those words that were so important to her, I suppose I should leave you with my own admonishment, my own hope, my own wish for you:

First, start with the HOPE that whatever is currently bothering you in the precious domains of your life of your health, mental health, relationships, career, finances, family, and community, that is creating a gap between how life is, and how you would like it to be, CAN be changed. Challenge any lingering idea that you are helpless, or that you don't "have it in you" to endure, succeed, and thrive. You do.

Use your internal and external resources. Challenge yourself to identify the thoughts, beliefs, and behaviors necessary to bring about meaningful and positive change.

Empower yourself. And have the life you want!

Epilogue: "The Last Good Fairy"

As a shy and sometimes bullied child who was often just plain not all that happy, I escaped into television and books. And among books, fairy tales. That was the section I'd run to in the elementary school library, and ask the librarian for new titles. My fascination with L. Frank Baum's *Oz* series is what I credit in part for keeping me sane through childhood enough to reach adulthood in the first place.

As I worked through graduate school as a social worker, I was reminded of one such fairy tale, Sleeping Beauty. The story tells of a kingdom where a treasured Princess Aurora is born, and a christening party is held for the all the "right" people on the guest list. This included three good fairies. The first fairy gave the baby Aurora the gift of beauty, in face and in heart, that she should inspire others always. The second fairy gave the baby Aurora the gift of happiness, that she should enjoy and share it.

Just then, the bad fairy arrived, angry at not being invited to the party. She, too, cast a "gift": a curse that the beautiful baby Aurora would prick her finger on a spindle by the eve of her sixteenth birthday, and die. Horrified, the family and guests recoiled at such a vile curse, and began to despair.

Just then, the last good fairy emerged, and urged all to hold and listen, for she had not yet given her gift. "I cannot remove the curse that has been given," she explained. "My powers to undo that are, alas, not that great. But I can do something," she encouraged. "The princess shall not prick her finger on the spindle and die, but she shall fall asleep, along with all here, until she is awakened by her True Love's kiss, who shall be a prince."

We all know how the story ends – the prince finds the sleeping beauty princess, awakens her with his kiss, and all awoke and lived happily ever after.

Psychotherapists are like that last good fairy. We can't use our powers of training, concern, theory, interpretation, advocacy, arbitration, intervention and compassion to completely remove all of the world's ills – illness, violence, abuse, tragedy, discrimination, domination, misfortune, crime, and blight. But, we can use the powers we have developed to mitigate these things, and to bring improvement to the people who have been affected by them.

That's my role, with each person I work with. I hear their story; I hear their "curse," and I recognize the gifts of their strengths that have been given by the good fairies before me. And I do what I can, to lift their curse and awaken them to a new life in love and peace.

References

Bass, Ellen, and Laura Davis. 1988. *The Courage to Heal: a Guide for Women Survivors of Child Sexual Abuse*. New York: Perennial Library.

Campbell, Chellie. 2002. *The Wealthy Spirit: Daily Affirmations for Financial Stress Reduction*. Naperville, IL: Source.

Canfield, Jack, and Janet Switzer. 2005. *The Success Principles: How to Get from Where You Are to Where You Want to Be*. New York: Harper Resource Book.

Carlson, Richard. 1997. *Don't Sweat the Small Stuff-- and It's All Small Stuff: Simple Ways to Keep the Little Things from Taking over Your Life*. New York: Hyperion.

Diagnostic and Statistical Manual of Mental Disorders, Fourth Edition: Primary Care Version. 1995. Washington, DC: American Psychiatric Association.

Forward, Susan, and Craig Buck. 1989. *Toxic Parents: Overcoming Their Hurtful Legacy and Reclaiming Your Life*. New York: Bantam.

Frankl, Viktor E. 1963. *Man's Search for Meaning; an Introduction to Logotherapy*. Boston: Beacon.

Fulghum, Robert. 1988. *Everything I Ever Really Needed to Know I Learned in Kindergarten*. Evanston, IL: Press of Ward Schori.

Grigsby, Charles, Donald Bauman, Steven E. Gregorich, and Cynthia Roberts-Gray. "Disaffiliation to Entrenchment: A Model for Understanding Homelessness." *Journal of Social Issues* 46.4 (1990): 141-56.

Grodzki, Lynn. 2000. *Building Your Ideal Private Practice: a Guide for Therapists and Other Healing Professionals*. New York: W.W. Norton.

Hay, Louise L. 1984. *Heal Your Body*. Santa Monica, CA. Hay House.

Hay, Louise L. 2005. *Receiving Prosperity*. Santa Monica, CA. Hay House.

Hay, Louise L. 1984. *You Can Heal Your Life*. Santa Monica, CA: Hay House.

Hendrix, Harville. 1988. *Getting the Love You Want: a Guide for Couples*. New York: H. Holt.

Hendrix, Harville. 1992. *Keeping the Love You Find: a Guide for Singles*. New York, NY: Pocket.

Hill, Napoleon. 1996. *Think and Grow Rich*. New York, NY: Ballantine.

Jeffers, Susan J. 1988. *Feel the Fear and Do It Anyway*. New York: Ballantine.

Levine, Judith. 2002. *Harmful to Minors: the Perils of Protecting Children from Sex*. Minneapolis: University of Minnesota.

Lew, Mike. 1990. *Victims No Longer: Men Recovering from Incest and Other Sexual Child Abuse*. New York: Perennial Library.

Orman, Suze. 2005. *The Money Book for the Young, Fabulous & Broke*. New York: Riverhead.

Shernoff, Michael. 1999. *AIDS and Mental Health Practice: Clinical and Policy Issues*. Binghamton, NY: Haworth.

Shernoff, Michael. 1997. *Gay Widowers: Life after the Death of a Partner*. New York: Haworth.

Siegel, Bernie S. 1986. *Love, Medicine, & Miracles: Lessons Learned about Self-healing from a Surgeon's Experience with Exceptional Patients*. New York: Harper & Row.

Terkel, Studs. 1974. *Working: People Talk about What They Do All Day and How They Feel about What They Do*. New York: Pantheon.

Truffo, Casey. 2007. *Be a Wealthy Therapist: Finally, You Can Make a Living While Making a Difference*. Saint Peters, MO: MP.

Index

Notes on Writing a Book

I think it's important to note that this book took a long time to write. Not just because the thoughts, feelings, opinions, and perspectives evolved over my forty-six years of life and nineteen years as a therapist by the time I wrote it, but also it took a long time because I procrastinated writing it because through much of it I worried about how it would be received. Would it be liked? How would it be evaluated? It was as if I were writing a term paper for a grade, or doing a triple-Lutz jump for an Olympic ice skating judge. But, I wasn't getting paid to write it. I didn't pay to take a course, which would have included paying a teacher who would grade me. I wrote this late at night, "on the edges of the day" as author Toni Morrison once said that she wrote her first books, in the mornings before the day really began, and late at night when the house was dark and quiet and the world seemed to sleep except for my flying fingers that jumped over the keyboard of my Dell PC the way other people were simultaneously seeing sheep jump over the fence as they drifted off in post-Midnight, Morpheus bliss.

I finally decided that this book is for me, and my expression and making sense of the things that I have come to observe, think, surmise, witness, posit, calculate, summate, experience, expunge, embrace, interpret, reflect, confront, reiterate, modify, clarify, challenge, refute, accept, and exalt in my years of clinical practice. Just writing this book is an act of "self-empowerment" – which is either appropriate, ironic, or something. How many people have been "afraid" to write a book because they weren't sure if it would be any good? How many have been afraid to write a song? Sing a song? Get a Mohawk? (I did that; it was great.) Change their makeup? Dye their hair? (I do that all the time.) Dye it back? (I do that, too.) Get a tattoo? Get a piercing? (No comment.) Go back to school? Quit school? Get a job? Change a job? Get into, or out of, a relationship? Paint the house? Redecorate? Change their minds? All this self-doubt and second-guessing all because they were afraid of *evaluation*. Evaluation can be useful, but I think it has its limitations and sometimes it's just plain overrated. Sometimes, self-empowerment means we need to do things for their own sake, not because of the chance for positive evaluation, and certainly not *avoiding* doing things because of a fear of negative evaluation.

This book is for those who can read it, get something out of it, and enjoy it. You're not paying to evaluate it; you're paying for the opportunity to read it. You're paying for the opportunity to come into someone else's mind. For those who like this book, it is a book. For those who do not like this book, it is a paperweight. Either way, it's something useful. Nothing is ever a waste.

Is there a book in *you*? I took the dare. I wrote mine. Now, it's your turn. Sing your song. Get your Mohawk. Write your book. Now, *that's* self-empowerment.

About the Author

Ken Howard, MSW, LCSW is a licensed psychotherapist and life/business/executive coach in private practice in West Hollywood, California. He specializes in working with gay male individuals and couples, but sees people from all walks of life. He also maintains a busy speaking schedule on various topics in inspiration and motivation. He lives in West Hollywood with his husband, cat, and dog. His websites include www.HaveTheLifeYouWant.com, www.GayTherapyLA.com, and www.PozTherapist.com.

Printed in Great Britain
by Amazon

85334464R00089